Passing the
Oxbridge Admissions Tests

Passing the Oxbridge Admissions Tests

Rosalie Hutton and Glenn Hutton

LearningMatters

Published by Learning Matters
33 Southernhay East
Exeter EX1 1NX
Tel: 01392 215560
info@learningmatters.co.uk
www.learningmatters.co.uk

First published in 2008 by Learning Matters Limited

British Cataloguing-in-Publication Data

A catalogue record for this book is available from the British Library.

ISBN 978 184445 185 2

Cover design by Topics – The Creative Partnership
Project Management by Swales & Willis Ltd
Typeset by Swales & Willis Ltd
Printed and bound in Great Britain by TJ International Ltd, Padstow, Cornwall

FSC
Mixed Sources
Product group from well-managed
forests and other controlled sources
Cert no. SGS-COC-2482
www.fsc.org
© 1996 Forest Stewardship Council

Contents

Preface

The University of Cambridge researched and developed the Thinking Skills Assessment (TSA), which has been in use since 2001, when the demand for some of their courses far outweighed availability and the University identified the need for a vehicle that would better identify applicants with an aptitude for success in higher education. The proliferation of applicants with high grades at A-level, and other factors, provided a problem for Cambridge in their selection process. It is expected that 27 of the 29 Cambridge Colleges will use the TSA for the purpose of determining admissions but they will only do so for some subjects; mainly Computer Science, Engineering and Economics, Land Economy, Natural Sciences, and Social and Political Sciences. Cambridge also use the Biomedical Admissions Test (BMAT) for entry to study medicine.

The University of Oxford have experienced similar issues to Cambridge, receiving approximately 1300 applications for a course that has around 250 places and the number of applications is growing annually. From 2007 students applying to Oxford to study Economics and Management, Philosophy, Politics and Economics are required to sit the TSA and undertake an additional Writing Task.

Oxford also have other admission tests including the National Admissions Test for Law (LNAT), United Kingdom Clinical Aptitude Test (UKCAT), and several other tests usually conducted at the interview stage. All these tests are discussed in more detail in Chapter 6 of the book.

The admissions tests for Oxford & Cambridge are designed to help admissions tutors to determine whether candidates have the skills and aptitudes that are required to study for their chosen degree, for example, the ability to think critically, reason analytically, and use language accurately and effectively.

Recent research has examined the predictive validity of the TSA for 1st year examination performance in Computer Science, Economics, Engineering, and Natural Sciences at the University of Cambridge. The research used three successive years of TSA and examination data. The findings indicated that the total scores of the TSA were a strong predictor of achieving both the highest and the lowest examination classes (*The predictive validity of the Thinking Skills Assessment: a combined analysis of three cohorts*, Joanne L. Emery, October 2007). This is reassuring in the sense that the tests do appear to be achieving their intended purpose.

The purpose of this book is essentially to provide a step-by-step guide to understanding critical reasoning tests, problem solving tests, and the elements of Oxford's Writing Task.

This book is the third in a series where universities have introduced pre-entry assessments in order to discriminate amongst applicants. The two previous books are concerned with the UK Clinical Aptitude Test (UKCAT) and Bio-Medical Admissions Test (BMAT), and the National Admissions Test for Law (LNAT). The UKCAT/BMAT is a test required for those applying to study medicine or dentistry, whilst the LNAT is for applicants intending to study law. Both these tests are discussed briefly in Chapter 6 of this book.

About the Authors

Rosalie Hutton is an Occupational Psychologist, specialising in the field of assessment and testing, who designs and publishes a range of psychological assessment measures. Critical reasoning and problem solving tests have been used commercially for a number of years in the recruitment and selection of staff and Rosalie provides the rationale for the use of these tests together with a developmental approach to understanding critical reasoning and problem solving type questions and how best to arrive at the correct answer. Rosalie is also the co-author of the other two books in this series.

Glenn Hutton has worked at a senior level in a major assessment organisation that tests several thousand people a year using multiple-choice type questions. During this time he had close links with the National Board of Medical Examiners in the United States which tests up to 100,000 doctors a year using online multiple-choice tests. Glenn is also a technical author for Oxford University Press annually producing manuals associated with the criminal law, and is co-author of the two other books in this series.

Chapter 1
Introduction

1. Oxbridge admissions tests

Both Oxford and Cambridge use the Thinking Skills Assessment (TSA) and Oxford also includes a second element where candidates are required to undertake a Writing Task.

The TSA results are not used in isolation and both universities consider other information available about each candidate including GCSE results and other qualifications, predicted grades for A-Level or equivalent, school reference, UCAS personal statement, samples of school work and interview performance, to assess potential and select applicants.

At Cambridge the TSA is taken at the time of interview in the UK and overseas and is administered under examination conditions with an invigilator present. Applicants do not need to do anything in terms of registering for the test as Cambridge Colleges will notify applicants of all admissions requirements.

To find out whether you will need to take the TSA at Oxford or Cambridge you are advised to look at the exact entry requirements for a particular course by referring to the University of Oxford and University of Cambridge websites.

2. How will this book help me?

This book has been produced to provide any person preparing for the TSA with an in-depth understanding of the assessment they will face.

Chapter 1 of the book examines your choice of applying to Oxford or Cambridge and the admissions process to these universities. The process outlined is simply a summary and is not intended to replace the informative websites provided by the universities (Oxford: www.ox.ac.uk – Cambridge: www.cam.ac.uk), or the *UCAS Big Guide 2009*. This UCAS book is really a **MUST** for any applicant, being the official universities and colleges entrance guide for 2009 entry. Two other useful and popular publications are, *MPW: Getting into Oxford and Cambridge* by Sarah Alajija, and *Oxbridge Entrance: The Real Rules* by Elfi Pallis.

Chapter 2 provides full details of the TSA requirements. This is followed by a clear explanation of the format and design of multiple-choice questions both generally and specific to the TSA.

Chapter 3 provides a step-by-step, developmental approach to answering problem-solving and critical thinking questions. By the end of this chapter you should have a good understanding of this type of assessment and how best to arrive at the correct answer.

Chapter 4 replicates the Thinking Skills Assessment. The chapter consists of 50 questions – 25 problem solving and 25 critical thinking. In the actual test the time allowed is 90 minutes and you might consider timing yourself against this constraint for some indication as to your level of performance. However, this practice test has not been written to be time constrained but as a vehicle: (a) to consolidate what has been learnt from the previous chapter, and (b) to give you confidence when dealing with such questions. Rather than simply giving the 'correct response', the answers to the practice test provide the rationale for both the correct and incorrect answers. This approach has proved to be effective in developing a person's knowledge and understanding of a particular subject.

Chapter 5 looks at the Writing Task requirement used by Oxford. This is not meant to be an exhaustive review of the skills required for this task but does consider style, structure, and the use of critical thinking skills, to enable you to write a well-reasoned piece of work in the time allowed.

Chapter 6 examines some of the other admissions tests used by Oxford and Cambridge.

In addition to the practice tests and information given here, there are other things that can be done to prepare for your admission to Oxford or Cambridge. Whilst it may seem very informal, one of the most effective ways, both to prepare for and succeed in your interview and study in higher education, is to read a 'quality' newspaper. In fact the universities recommend this.

This book does not claim to be able to help you do well in the test but it should speed up your reactions and give you confidence in the style of questions you will encounter.

3. Application process for Oxford and Cambridge

The application process for Oxford and Cambridge starts earlier than other universities. Your UCAS application must be submitted by **mid-October** for entry in 2009 (or for deferred entry in 2010) so that there is time to arrange the interview process. UCAS accept applications from the beginning of **September**.

For Oxford you will also need to complete an Oxford Application Form, and return it to the Undergraduate Admissions Office by post by **mid-October**. The application deadlines and admissions test arrangements may be different for candidates applying from outside the EU.

In the past all applicants to Cambridge were asked to submit a Cambridge Application Form in addition to a UCAS application. It is planned that applicants from the UK and EU for 2009 entry (or deferred entry in 2010) will only need to submit a UCAS application in order to apply to Cambridge. If you are applying from outside the EU, you will need to submit a Cambridge Overseas Application Form (COAF) in addition to your UCAS application. However, once your application has been received you will be asked to provide additional information through a Supplementary Application Questionnaire (SAQ).

Both Oxford and Cambridge, depending on your intended course of study, may require you to provide one or two samples of academic work for tutors to assess.

Also, you may already know this, but if you don't, you cannot apply to Oxford and Cambridge in the same year.

Educational requirements

Oxford
Conditional offers are likely to be for high grades, and may specify certain grades to be achieved in particular subjects if they have not been achieved already. Oxford University does not have any formal matriculation requirements, and no requirement for any particular subjects or grades at GCSE. Providing that you meet any specific requirements for your course, the university recommend you to take those subjects that interest you most and in which you feel you have the ability to do best – '*tutors are much more interested in candidates' overall academic ability, and their potential and motivation . . ., than the particular programmes which have been followed at school.*'

Cambridge
Cambridge have minimum entrance requirements for all applicants regardless of course and age. These requirements are designed to ensure you have had a sufficiently broad general education. Qualifications are required in English, a language other than English, an approved mathematical or scientific subject, and two other approved subjects. At least two of these subjects must be at A level and the others at GCSE (grades A, B or C). If , for example, you have not taken a language other than English at GCSE, this requirement may be waived by the admissions tutor where considered aporopriate.

For both Universities, conditional offers for A-level students are likely to be AAA, and providing that any specific subject requirements have been met, all A-levels are approved for admissions purposes. However, General Studies and Critical Thinking A-levels will only be considered as fourth A-level subjects and will not therefore be accepted as part of a conditional offer.

All teaching at Oxford and Cambridge is carried out in English (with the exception of some language-specific teaching) and non-native English-speaking applicants must convince tutors that they have sufficient fluency in written and spoken English to cope with their course.

Even only accepting applicants with A grades at A-level makes it difficult for tutors to assess and choose students on that basis alone. Hence, additional forms of assessment, which are the subject of this book, have been introduced in an effort to make selection as fair as possible.

Writing your personal statement

Before offering a place, Oxford and Cambridge are looking at three main things: your exam results, your referee's statement and your personal statement. Exam results and referees' statements seldom help universities to make selection decisions, whereas the personal statement is your opportunity to convince the university to offer you a place. They want to see that you will fit into university life, not just academically but socially as well.

Apart from telling the reader of your personal statement why you want to study at Oxford or Cambridge you should also include information about your work experience, volunteer work, academic commitment and extracurricular activities.

Work experience can often be difficult for those of you who are coming straight from full-time education but access schemes at weekends and during holidays are often available especially in the A2 year. However, do not be dismayed if you have problems gaining work experience; universities are aware of how difficult this can be.

Volunteer work is considered by many as important in the sense that it demonstrates a commitment to helping others in the community and develops your people and softer skills. Getting involved is easy and you should look for something you would enjoy and that you might stick at for months or longer. Lots of volunteering positions only require up to four hours commitment a week and with some there are opportunities to attend training courses, e.g. first aid. Careers advisers may be able to help organise volunteer work or you can visit the following websites: www.volunteering.org.uk (this is the Volunteering England site and contains information and addresses); www.do-it.org.uk (this is 'volunteering made easy'; just enter your address and the type of project you want to get involved with). So if you aren't volunteering you might consider it's time to get off your bum and start to help others – oh and by the way, it can be FUN and it's FREE!

Academic commitment means demonstrating that you understand the commitment required for the hard work you will face to complete your degree and beyond. Your exam results do not amply demonstrate your commitment to studying, but reading up on an area of your intended degree that might interest you would – so make a note of everything you read outside your A-level course work in preparation for completing the personal statement.

Extracurricular activities are important as these provide evidence that you are a well-rounded person with a number of hobbies and interests. This may include playing representative sport, being a member of a society, a musician, or undertaking the Duke of Edinburgh Awards scheme. Where possible showing positions of responsibility are beneficial to demonstrate your leadership skills and the fact that you are confident and willing to undertake such responsibilities.

The importance of the personal statement cannot be overstated. You need to start it early in the application process and ensure it is providing the best impression of yourself, your skills and your ambitions. No doubt you will not be completely alone in preparing the statement as teachers and tutors take considerable interest in its preparation.

Interviews

The Oxford and Cambridge websites contain detailed information on interviews, what to expect, how to prepare and even what to wear. Consequently, the following provides just a basic outline of the interview process. Remember, the interview is just one aspect of your application, as tutors will also consider your examination results, personal statement, academic reference, predicted grades, and admissions tests or written work (where required).

The interview is designed to assess your academic abilities and, most importantly, your academic potential. It not only provides tutors with an opportunity to evaluate your understanding of, and aptitude for, your subject, but also gives you the opportunity to explain why you are committed to your proposed course of study. It is important to note that whether or not you are accepted will be based on your academic abilities and potential, not your manners or etiquette, appearance, or background.

In a nutshell you will be required to demonstrate your:

- academic ability
- capacity to deal with the rigors of the course

- logic and reasoning ability
- knowledge of current affairs, especially those concerning the course.

These areas are really what you would expect, and the last point reiterates the benefits of reading around your chosen subject by regularly reading a 'quality' newspaper, journals, magazines and other relative publications.

Chapter 2
Multiple-choice questions

4. Thinking Skills Assessment

The Thinking Skills Assessment (TSA) is designed to help Oxford and Cambridge to make more informed choices amongst the many highly qualified applicants who apply for some of their degree programmes. The test has been designed to assess the ability of individuals to think critically and reason analytically, traits that identify individuals who are more likely to succeed in higher education.

The TSA is an assessment of two kinds of thinking: problem solving – reasoning using numerical and spatial skills, and critical thinking – reasoning using everyday written language.

The assessment consists of 50 multiple-choice questions within a time constraint of 90 minutes. The test is normally pencil and paper, although facilities do exist for it to be conducted online. Where the test is pencil and paper a soft pencil (HB or softer) and a good eraser are essential. All of the 50 questions must be attempted and these vary in difficulty from easy to very hard. There are 25 problem-solving questions and 25 critical thinking questions that are mixed throughout the question paper. The reason for this is to ensure candidates complete a sufficient number of each type of question should they not complete the full test in the time allotted. It is recommended that candidates work steadily through the test from start to finish rather than jump around. Calculators are NOT permitted, but dictionaries (book or electronic) are, although this provision is primarily aimed at candidates whose first language is not English.

The additional Writing Task required by Oxford is allocated 30 minutes and candidates are provided with three essay questions from which they select one. The essay questions are on general subjects that do not require any specialised knowledge. The purpose of the Writing Task is to afford candidates an opportunity to show that they can communicate effectively in writing, organising their ideas and presenting them clearly and concisely.

In relation to the problem-solving element of the TSA a curriuculum is provided by Cambridge Assessment and this is reproduced in Chapter 3.

However, in respect of the critical thinking element of the TSA, designers of similar tests, e.g. UKCAT/BMAT and LNAT, will maintain that the tests do not contain any curriculum, nor any science content, nor can it be revised for. Tests like the UKCAT and LNAT, together with the critical thinking element of the test being presented by Cambridge Assessment, have been in existence for many decades and are used widely in the selection, assessment and development of staff. None of these commercially available tests claim to have any curriculum or science content and cannot specifically be revised for. However, it has been demonstrated that familiarisation in understanding and practising such tests does increase both levels of competence and performance. It also helps to reduce anxiety levels as applicants are not faced with the unknown.

5. Format and design of multiple-choice questions

This section provides a brief overview of multiple-choice question tests and then examines their format and design and in particular that being used in the TSA.

Which of the following are true of multiple-choice tests and questions?

A   The tests are very simplistic

B   The questions are easy to answer

C   The tests are a poor substitute for real examinations

D   A good guessing strategy will always get you a decent mark

E   None of the above

The answer, of course, is E – none of the above.

Multiple-choice tests have a very good track record in the field of assessment and particularly in selection. Multiple-choice questions are a technique that simply tests the candidates' knowledge and understanding of a particular subject on the date of the test. They make candidates read and think but *not write* about the question set, as is the case with essay-type questions.

It is true that there have been a number of long-held criticisms – and myths – about multiple-choice tests. For one, it has been a criticism that they are too simple-minded and trivial. What this observation really means is that it is perfectly obvious to the candidate what they have to do. There are no marks for working out what the examiner wants – it's obvious. But this is not the same as saying that the *answer* is obvious, far from it. In addition, multiple-choice questions are often referred to by students as being 'multiple-guess' questions, on the basis that the right answer lies in one of the options given and therefore you have a good mathematical chance of happening upon the right answer. Although systematic and even completely random guessing does occur in multiple-choice tests, their effects can be minimised and their use identified by properly constructed, presented and timed tests. The people who design and analyse multiple-choice tests are often just as interested in what *wrong* answers you give as the right ones. This is because, apart from other things, patterns can be discerned and compared with those of others taking the same test and tendencies towards certain answers (e.g. always choosing option B) will stand out.

In short, guessing is easy to spot and unlikely to succeed. Given that the purpose of the TSA is to inform the overall decision-making process in selecting you over your fellow applicants (rather than simply achieving a bad result or score) relying on guesswork is a poor strategy.

Multiple-choice tests are used extensively both in Europe and the USA, from staged tests in schools through to university selection and assessment, to some of the most complex and high-stake professional trade qualifications.

The strength of these tests is that they can provide fair and objective testing on a huge scale at small cost, in the sense that their administration is standardised and their developers can demonstrate that the results are not going to vary according to the marker, a criticism of essay-type tests.

The format and design of the multiple-choice questions used for the TSA will undoubtedly follow the general educational model.

The following descriptions of the format and design of multiple-choice questions are taken from two publications. Firstly, *Assessment and Testing: A survey of research*; University of Cambridge Local Examinations Syndicate (1995). The University of Cambridge Local Examinations Syndicate has been in existence for well over 100 years and prepares examinations for over 100 countries. Second, *Constructing Written Test Questions For the Basic Clinical Sciences* (Second Edition, Susan M Case and David B Swanson, National Board of Medical Examiners, 1998). The National Board of Medical Examiners, which is based in the USA, uses multiple-choice questions to test in excess of 100,000 medical students each year, including foreign doctors, at numerous sites throughout the world.

In all, multiple-choice testing properly conducted is well established, well used across the professional assessment world and well respected, none more so than Cambridge Assessment.

There are a number of different formats that can be used for multiple-choice tests but the most common format is that taken from the 'One Best Answer' family. Generally, this is the format used in the TSA and is discussed in detail below in relation to numerical/spatial tests and critical thinking tests. However, before looking at the TSA it is useful to understand the general structure of the 'One Best Answer' format.

'One Best Answer' format

The 'One Best Answer' format, also known as A-type questions, are the most widely used in multiple-choice tests. They make explicit the number of choices to be selected and *usually* consist of a **stem**, a ***lead-in question***, followed by a series of ***choices***, normally between three and five choices. To demonstrate this we will use a simple example taken from a typical numerical aptitude test.

Stem

The **stem** is usually a set of circumstances that can be presented in a number of different ways. The circumstances may be presented in a few simple sentences, as a document, a letter, some form of pictorial display or may be longer passages, such as newspaper articles, extracts from books or periodicals. It provides all the information for the question that will follow.

A simple numerical aptitude **stem** could be:

> *A college had 20,000 students in 2007. 8,000 of the students studied a science subject.*

Lead-in question

The ***lead-in question*** identifies the exact answer the examiner requires from the circumstances provided in the **stem**.

For example, the ***lead-in question*** for the **stem** example given above could be:

> *What is the approximate ratio of students studying science to the total number of students at the college?*

Choices

The ***choices*** provided will always consist of ONE correct answer with the remainder being incorrect answers; these incorrect answers are referred to as 'distracters'.

For example, typical ***choices*** for the **stem** and ***lead-in question*** example given above could be:

A 2:3

B 2:5

C 3:2

D 3:5

E 4:2

Answer and rationale

Ratio: rule
A **ratio** allows one quantity to be compared with another quantity. Any two numbers can be compared by writing them alongside each other with the numbers being separated by a ratio sign (:).

Answer: B is correct – 2:5

Step 1: write the figures separated by the ratio sign with the number being compared first, so here 8,000:20,000

Step 2: reduce these figures down if possible. Here they can be reduced to 8:20 by discounting the thousands and then further reduced by dividing both numbers by 4 to obtain 2:5.

Step 3: the ratio of students studying science compared with the total number of students at the college is 2:5.

The areas being tested by the TSA, Problem Solving and Critical Thinking, are dealt with separately in Chapter 3.

6. Format of the Thinking Skills Assessment: problem solving

This part of the test assesses your ability to solve numerical and spatial problems. The format is very similar to that described in the numerical aptitude example given above.

Stem
The *stem* will consist of tables, charts, and/or graphs.

Lead-in question
For each of the stems, i.e. the tables, charts, and/or graphs, there will be one **lead-in question**.

Choices
There will be five *choices* for each question, A, B, C, D and E. Remember, there is only ONE correct answer and the remaining four choices will be 'distracters', i.e. incorrect.

7. Format of the Thinking Skills Assessment: critical thinking

This part of the test assesses your ability to think logically about written information and arrive at a reasoned conclusion.

The format of the critical thinking part of the test is similar to that described to the example given above, with the exception being that the *lead-in question* actually becomes a *statement*. This is explained further in Chapter 3.

Stem
The *stem* will consist of short passages of text.

Lead-in question
For each of the stems, i.e. the passages of text, there will be one **lead-in question**.

Choices
There will be five possible *choices* for each question, A, B, C, D and E. Only ONE of these choices will be the correct answer and the remaining four choices will be 'distracters'.

8. How to approach multiple-choice questions

Whatever the purpose or design of the test, it is worth bearing in mind some general rules to follow when answering multiple-choice questions. Clearly, your score should be higher if you attempt to answer all of the questions in the test and avoid wild guessing. However, if you are running out of time you may attempt some 'educated' guesses but where five options are available this may prove difficult. If there are questions you are unsure of you can return to them later.

Although it is often repeated at every level of testing and assessment in every walk of life, it is nevertheless worth reiterating – **always read the questions carefully**. It may help to read them more than once to avoid misreading a critical word(s).

Where all the options, or some of the options, begin with the same word(s), or appear very similar, be sure to mark the correct option.

When undertaking a multiple-choice test such as the TSA there are essentially two strategies that can be adopted:

Strategy 1

Carefully read the passage, then read each question and then go on to examine each of the options in turn to see whether it is possibly correct or whether it can be eliminated. This process of elimination should leave you with the correct answer. However, you should be aware that you might become more susceptible to the distracters and immediately believe one to be the correct answer. In relation to critical thinking questions you may then go through a process of 'justifying' your choice to yourself and therefore not have an open mind to conflicting arguments elsewhere in the passage.

This strategy is the more conventional approach that would probably be followed by most test takers.

Strategy 2

Carefully read the passage and then attempt each question *without looking at the options available*. When you have arrived at a possible answer for the question you can examine the options to see if your choice, or a close match, is available. This process would validate or invalidate your answer thus allowing you to move on or review your answer.

Alternatively, you may read the question first and then carefully read the passage in an attempt to arrive at a possible answer before looking at the options.

This is a more deliberate strategy and feels less 'intuitive' than the first strategy above.

It is of course a matter of personal choice which of the two strategies you adopt. However, in either case, an initial skim read of the passage might be beneficial.

In relation to the critical thinking questions **do not use your own knowledge or experience** of the subject matter to influence your answers even if your knowledge contradicts that of the writer. The concept of this part of the test is not to test individual prior knowledge – it is to present everyone competing against you with the same opportunity to demonstrate their skills and aptitudes. As such your answers should relate directly to:

1. *your understanding of the passage you have read* and
2. *the way in which the writer has presented it to you, the reader.*

Examine each passage to extract the main ideas and avoid drawing hasty conclusions.

The following two chapters of the book contain details of the TSA problem-solving and critical thinking elements and provides a practice test covering each of these areas. By working through these chapters you will not only familiarise yourself with the format of these tests but speed up your reactions and give yourself the confidence successfully to handle the differing style of questions involved.

9. Problem solving

The problem-solving part of the TSA assesses a candidate's ability to solve numerical and spatial problems. It requires the candidate to solve problems by extracting relevant information from tables and other numerical presentations. It assumes familiarity with numbers to a good pass at GCSE but the problems to be solved are less to do with numerical facility and more to do with problem solving (i.e. knowing what information to use and how to manipulate it using simple calculations and ratios). Hence, it measures reasoning using numbers as a vehicle, rather than measuring a facility with numbers.

Commercially produced numerical aptitude tests have been in existence for many years mainly for use in the selection and assessment of staff. There have been numerous books written on how to pass or how to master these types of psychometric tests, and what follows is a précis on what you need to consider specifically in approaching this part of the test. Essentially, the advice on preparation for any aptitude test, contained in Chapter 2, holds true for numerical/ spatial tests.

Quite simply, numerical and spatial tests are designed to measure your ability to understand numbers and visualise shapes in different dimensions and rotations. The numerical part of the test relates to the four basic arithmetic operations of addition, subtraction, multiplication and division, as well as number sequences and simple mathematics. Therefore, in preparing for such tests you need to be able to perform simple calculations without the use of a calculator.

This chapter provides you with an opportunity to test your understanding and knowledge of the range of numerical and spatial questions you are likely to be presented with in the TSA. By taking this opportunity you should be able to identify any numerical areas where you may need some development. Obviously, as with any other type of examination, numerical questions can be presented in a variety of different ways. However, the basic computations used will always be the same. So learn or remind yourself of the basics! The example questions provided in this chapter not only include the correct answer and rationale but also the reasons why the other options are incorrect. In addition, this section also provides the 'mathematical rule' for each question. All this is designed to reinforce or build on your understanding and knowledge of the syllabus areas.

10. Problem-solving curriculum

Twenty-five of the 50 questions contained in the TSA are numerical/spatial items associated with tables, charts and/or graphs. These questions are mixed with the critical thinking questions throughout the question paper.

The curriculum for mathematical knowledge and skill, covered in the problem-solving part of the assessment, is provided by Cambridge Assessment (© UCLES 2003) as follows:

Number concepts
- simple fractions
- place value (for example, knowing that the '5' in '7654' indicates '50')
- ideas about percentages (for example, the idea that 1% could be thought of as '1 in every 100', and that if 20% of a group of adults are men, 80% must be women)

Numerical operations
- the four rules of number (addition, subtraction, multiplication, division)
- percentage operations (for example, if something was sold at £10, and is now advertised at '20% off', how much would the customer pay?)
- calculations in everyday contexts (complex calculations with fractions and decimals are not required)

Quantities
- time and the calendar
- money
- measures including:
  length – kilometre (km), metre (m), centimetre (cm), millimetre (mm)
  weight – kilogramme (kg), gramme (g)
  area – square centimetre, square metre
  volume (capacity) – cubic centimetre, litre (l), gallons

Note
Knowledge of the following relationships is also required:

1 km = 1000 m, 1 m = 100 cm, 1 cm = 10 mm, 1 kg = 1000 g

You are also required to know the terms for measurements that are used informally in daily life (e.g. feet, miles), but numerical relationships for these measures (e.g. 12 inches = 1 foot) are not required.

Space and spatial reasoning
- area (including the calculation of the area of a rectangle)
- perimeter (including calculation)
- volume (including the calculation of the volume of a box)
- reflections (in mirrors) and rotations of simple shapes
- two-dimensional (2D) representations of three-dimensional (3D) shapes (for example, being able to interpret a 'bird's eye view' of a house)

Generalisation
- recognition that some operations are generalisable, for example that converting 24 to 3 and 40 to 5 both involve division by 8 (formal algebra is not required)

Tables and graphs
- extracting information from graphs
- extracting information from tables

Note
The above is the full curriculum that *may* be used in the TSA – because of the limitation in relation to the number of questions in the test (25) not all of the curriculum will be contained in each test.

11. Problem-solving example questions

The type of format used in problem-solving questions is the same as that used as an example of multiple-choice questions in the previous chapter. That is a *stem* in the form of a table, chart or graph, followed by a *lead-in question* and then five possible *choices* – A, B, C, D or E.

Example question

The following example requires you to select the correct answer from the five options provided. The rationale for the correct and incorrect answers is provided after the question.

The table below shows the miles travelled by a sales representative.

	Mon	Tue	Wed	Thu	Fri	Sat
WEEK 1	197.5	189	213.5	231	190	437
WEEK 2	116.5	145	202	173	52	

You want to find her median mileage over the 11 days.

Which of these would you do?

A Find the sixth number and divide this by 2.

B Add all the numbers together and divide by 11.

C Rearrange the numbers into numerical order and then find the sixth number.

D Find the average for each week and divide this by 2.

E Add the two middle numbers together and divide this by 2.

Example question: answer and rationale

Median: rule
The **median** of a distribution is the middle value when the values are arranged in order. When there are two middle values (i.e. for an even number of values) then you add the two middle numbers and divide by 2. The highlighted statement and rationale is correct.

A **Find the sixth number and divide this by 2.**

This answer is incorrect as the method of finding the median does not entail dividing any of the individual values by 2.

B **Add all the numbers together and divide by 11.**

This answer is incorrect providing the method for finding the *mean* not the median.

C **Rearrange the numbers into numerical order and then find the sixth number.**

This answer is correct.

Step 1: arrange the 11 values in order – so 52, 116.5, 145, 173, 189, 190, 197.5, 202, 213.5, 231, 437.

Step 2: there are an odd number of values, so the median is the middle value, i.e. 190

D   Find the average for each week and divide this by 2.

This answer is incorrect as it is not a method for finding any type of average.

E   Add the two middle numbers together and divide this by 2.

This answer is incorrect providing the method for finding the *median* when dealing with an even number of values.

The questions used by Cambridge Assessment are of three specific kinds: Relevant Selection, Finding Procedures, and Identifying Similarity. Below are three examples, answers and rationale of these types of question.

Relevant Selection

Example question
The table below shows the dimensions and prices of various estate cars. I want to buy an estate car for both private and trade use. I am a plumber by trade and need to carry copper pipe in the luggage space up to a length of 1.2 m that for security reasons I want to keep inside the vehicle. I also want to garage my car to prevent it being broken into. My garage is 3.2 m long and 2.25 m wide.

What is the lowest price estate car to satisfy these conditions?

Make	Ford	Peugeot	Fiat	VW
Length	2.8 m	2.5 m	2.6 m	3.25 m
Width	1.48 m	1.36 m	1.38 m	1.50 m
Interior length	1.8 m	1.75 m	1.70 m	2.10 m
Interior width	1.40 m	1.70 m	1.35 m	1.45 m
Luggage space	1.2 m	1.05 m	1.3 m	1.4 m
Private use**	£12,585	£11,995	£12,399	£12,495
Trade use	£10,333	£9,500	£10,459	£10,800

** Private use includes trade use

A   £10,333

B   £10,800

C   £11,995

D   £12,399

E   £12,585

Example question: answer and rationale

'Relevant Selection' means finding the required information from a majority of text that is redundant in achieving the solution, i.e. selecting those parts of the question that are relevant to achieving the correct answer. The highlighted statement and rationale is correct.

A   £10,333

This answer is incorrect as it is the trade price of the Ford and the requirement is a vehicle for private and trade use.

B   £10,800

This answer is incorrect as it is the trade price of the VW and the requirement is a vehicle for private and trade use. Also the VW at 3.25 m is too long for the garage at 3.2 m.

C   £11,995

This answer is incorrect as the luggage space of the Peugeot at 1.05 m is too small for the copper pipe at 1.2 m.

D   £12,399

This answer is correct. We need to find an estate car that will fit in a garage 3.2 m long and 2.25 m wide and which will carry copper pipe in the luggage space up to a length of 1.2 m. The car is for both private and trade use. Both the Fiat and the Ford fit the specifications but the Fiat is cheaper.

E   £12,585

This answer is incorrect even though the Ford fits all the specifications it is more expensive than the Fiat for private use.

2. Finding Procedures

Example question

Mr Ahmed is replacing his fencing around the perimeter of his house. On the back fence overlooking fields he intends to use three lengths of wooden rails across the total length; on the two sides of the garden two lengths of wooden rails across the total length; on the front garden fence three lengths of wooden rails across the total length. The back fence measures 50 m; each side of the garden measures 45 m; the length of the front garden fence is 48 m which includes a 1 m wide gate. The wooden rails are 3 m long.

How many wooden rails will Mr Ahmed need to undertake all the fencing?

A   127 rails

B   142 rails

C   157 rails

D   158 rails

E   187 rails

Example question: answer and rationale

Multi-stage calculations: rule
'Finding procedures' relates to those occasions when you have abstracted the relevant information but are required to use a method or procedure to find the solution. The highlighted statement and rationale is correct.

A   127 rails

This answer is incorrect as it has used the calculation $45 \times 2 = 90/3 = 30$ rails; it has not doubled the number of rails for the two sides of the garden fence, i.e. $45 \times 2 \times 2 = 180/3 = 60$ rails

B   142 rails

This answer is incorrect as it has multiplied the front garden fence by 2 and not by 3 and has not deducted the 3 m for the gate.

C   157 rails

This answer is correct.

The calculation to arrive at this answer is:

$50 \times 3 \ (150) + 45 \times 2 \ (90) + 45 \times 2 \ (90) + 48 \times 3 \ (144) - 3 \ (141) = 471.$

Total length = 471 m divided by length of each rail = $471/3 = 157$ rails.

D   158 rails

This answer is incorrect as it has failed to deduct the 3 m for the gate in the front garden fence.

E   187 rails

This answer is incorrect as it has multiplied the side fencing of 2×45 m by 3 instead of 2.

Identifying Similarities

Example question

Bill is laying a gravel driveway that measures 20 m long and 4 m wide. He has calculated that he will require 0.05 tonnes of 20 mm gravel to cover one square metre of driveway. Bill therefore requires $80 \times 0.05 = 4$ tonnes of gravel.

Which of the following uses the same method of calculation as that above?

A   Sarah is paid £5.25 an hour to clean at the school. She works 3 hours a day for 4 days and 2 hours on Fridays. She earns £73.50 a week.

B   To lay a lawn measuring 10.0 m by 6.0 m will require 15 kg of lawn seed where 0.25 kg of seed covers an area of one square metre.

C   Lucy puts 60 litres of petrol in her car. The next week she travels 360 miles before the car is empty. Lucy's car does 6 miles to the litre.

D   A 5 litre can of paint covers 15 square metres. Ranjit paints a 5.0 m by 4.0 m wall and a 5.0 m by 5.0 m ceiling. Ranjit needs three cans of paint.

E   Victor's company car business mileage for June is 1,500 miles and the total mileage is 2,300 miles. His private mileage for June is 800 miles.

Example question: answer and rationale

Identifying Similarities is simply matching the information provided with other information that is similar.

In matching the information provided; the procedure multiplies 80 (20×4) $\times$ 0.05 based on the size of the drive (20 m by 4 m) by the amount of gravel @ 0.05 tonnes per square metre. The highlighted statement and rationale is correct.

A   **Sarah is paid £5.25 an hour to clean at the school. She works 3 hours a day for 4 days and 2 hours on Fridays. She earns £73.50 a week.**

This answer is incorrect as it multiplies (3×4) + (3×2) $\times$ 5.25 thereby using a different procedure, i.e. method of calculation.

B   **To lay a lawn measuring 10.0 m by 6.0 m will require 15 kg of lawn seed where 0.25 kg of seed covers an area of one square metre.**

This answer is correct.

This answer uses the same procedure, i.e. multiplying 60 (10×6) by the amount of lawn seed @ 0.25 kg per square metre.

C   Lucy puts 60 litres of petrol in her car. The next week she travels 360 miles before the car is empty. Lucy's car does 6 miles to the litre.

This answer is incorrect as it divides 360 by 60 thereby using a different procedure, i.e. method of calculation.

D   A 5 litre can of paint covers 15 square metres. Ranjit paints a 5.0 m by 4.0 m wall and a 5.0 m by 5.0 m ceiling. Ranjit needs three cans of paint.

This answer is incorrect as it multiplies 5×4 by 5×5 and divides by 5 thereby using a different procedure, i.e. method of calculation.

E   Victor's company car business mileage for June is 1,500 miles and the total mileage is 2,300 miles. His private mileage for June is 800 miles.

This answer is incorrect as it subtracts 1,500 from 2,300 thereby using a different procedure, i.e. method of calculation.

12. Critical thinking

The notion that we all have 'thinking skills' or 'core skills' that should be transferable to all subject areas has attracted a great deal of academic interest. One of these 'core skills' is called 'critical thinking' and the vast number of books on the subject testifies to the interest in – and complexity of – the subject. Critical thinking is fundamentally concerned with the way arguments are structured and produced by whatever media; discussion, debate, a paper, a report, an article or an essay. The following are the generally accepted criteria for critical thinking:

- the ability to differentiate between facts and opinions
- the ability to examine assumptions
- being open minded as you search for explanations, causes and solutions
- being aware of valid or invalid argument forms
- staying focused on the whole picture, while examining the specifics
- verifying sources
- deducing and judging inductions
- inducing and judging inductions
- making value judgements
- defining terms and judging definitions
- deciding on actions
- being objective
- a willingness and ability always to look at alternatives

The list on page 23 is not meant to be an exhaustive list of all the criteria of critical thinking but it provides an overview of some of the basic principles that underpin the TSA. Applying your own critical reasoning, you will realise at this point that some of the criteria listed will lend themselves more readily to the TSA multiple-choice questions while others may be more relevant to the TSA Writing Task.

The fact that universities are now looking at setting aptitude tests (such as the TSA) that involve critical thinking skills, reflects the recognition that critical thinking is now being promoted in education generally. There is now an AS-level course (offered by the OCR Examination Board) in critical thinking. The course has five major areas: identifying the elements of reasoning; evaluating reasoning; recognising and evaluating assumptions; clarifying expressions and ideas; presenting a reasoned case in a clear, logical and coherent way. The assessment for this AS-level is by examination; there is no course work element and the examination is of similar format to the TSA, i.e. questions related to passages and essays.

In the commercial field, professional psychometric testing has for many years employed critical reasoning tests for similar reasons, i.e. the need for organisations to recruit or promote the right people, with the right skills, etc. In today's economic climate competition for jobs and training is intense and all the applicants find themselves in a selection pool of similarly qualified people, presenting a problem, not only for the applicant, but also for those who have a limited number of training places or job vacancies to offer. This makes the selection process difficult – from both perspectives. The result has been that the psychometrics profession, which comprises mainly test developers and publishers, has grown into a multi-million pound industry. Test developers are usually psychologists who specialise in testing (psychometrists) and it is usually their remit to construct tests of aptitude such as verbal, numerical, spatial ability, etc., as well as tests of other characteristics, such as personality.

When making selection decisions – whether they are for training, further education or for job appointments – the area of critical thinking/reasoning is deemed to be very important. This is largely because these skills are important in performing the roles themselves, particularly those in management. Graduate/managerial level aptitude tests of verbal reasoning, which are basically assessing the understanding of words, grammar, spelling, word relationships, etc. may provide an objective assessment of a candidate's verbal ability. However, these types of test are seen by some to lack face validity (that is, they do not appear to be job related) when used for graduate/managerial roles. People of this level often object to being given 'IQ tests' and prefer an assessment that appears to replicate, to some extent, the content of the job, i.e. critically evaluating reports. It is also believed by some that classic verbal reasoning tests do not provide an indication of an individual's ability to think critically, therefore psychometrists have developed what are generally called critical reasoning tests, which are similar in format to the TSA and described in the following section.

13. Critical thinking: example questions

Cambridge Assessment makes use of seven different types of question in the Thinking Skills element of the TSA and an explanation of these is provided below.

1. Summarising the main conclusion

Example question
A professional football club is considering screening players to determine whether they have a genetic disposition to be the next David Beckham or Steven Gerrard. Research has provided evidence that genetic experiments on mice and rats has identified enhanced physical performance and that it is likely this could translate to humans. Also a study in America compared versions of the ACTN3 gene among a number of athletes and found that elite performers were more likely to have particular combinations of this gene variant. It is claimed that people with one version of the ACTN3 gene would excel as sprinters whilst those with another version would be better at endurance events.

What is the **main conclusion** of this passage?

A   Professional footballers may be genetically screened to identify potential David Beckhams or Steven Gerrards.

B   Genetic screening could have a role to play in identifying athletic talent.

C   Enhanced physical performance equates to enhanced athletic skills.

D   Potential sprinters and endurance athletes will be easier to identify with genetic screening.

E   The ACTN3 gene can identify future athletic talent.

Example question: answer and Rationale
This question requires you to identify the **main conclusion** that can be drawn from the passage. A **conclusion** is simply a statement that is logical, that is a proposition that is arrived at after consideration of the evidence, arguments or premises. You are looking for the **main conclusion** that will follow from or be supported by the passage itself. The highlighted statement and rationale is correct.

A   Professional footballers may be genetically screened to identify potential David Beckhams or Steven Gerrards.

This is an incorrect answer as it picks up on the first part of the passage and does not take account of the other issues and evidence raised.

> **B   Genetic screening could have a role to play in identifying athletic talent.**
>
> This is the correct answer as the passage relates to two pieces of research both of which are concerned with genetic disposition providing evidence of an individual's level of athletic performance, to identify better performers. These are only research studies and therefore the **main conclusion** following from and supported by the passage is that genetic screening *could* have a role to play in identifying athletic talent.

C   Enhanced physical performance equates to enhanced athletic skills.

This is an incorrect answer as it cannot be concluded from the content of the passage. Although it is being suggested that enhanced physical performance can equate to enhanced athletic skills this may only be the case where combinations of the ACTN3 gene variant exist. Other variants may still enhance physical performance but not necessarily enhance athleticism.

D   Potential sprinters and endurance athletes will be easier to identify with genetic screening.

This is an incorrect answer as although this may be what the passage is suggesting and could be used as the main conclusion it is not the best answer available. The answer only reflects part of the content of the passage and is not as comprehensive a conclusion as that contained in the correct answer.

E   The ACTN3 gene can identify future athletic talent.

This is an incorrect answer as it is almost stating conclusively that the ACTN3 gene can identify future athletic talent whereas the passage relates to two research studies; the first only being used on mice and rats; the second stating that 'elite performers were *more likely* to have particular combinations of this gene variant'. It is therefore *likely* that people without the gene variant may be elite performers.

2. Drawing a conclusion

Example question

The Department for Children, Schools and Families plans to include eighteen social targets in Ofsted reports. It is suggested that schools would become broadly responsible for their pupils safety, enjoyment and happiness. The social targets would require schools to keep records of matters such as drug problems, teenage pregnancy rates, criminal records, obesity levels, bullying, etc. The findings would be published in Ofsted's annual report which is widely used by parents to find out more about their child's school or when selecting a school in their area. The targets would also help to highlight differences between primary and secondary schools in similar circumstances.

Which one of the following conclusions is best supported by the passage?

A   Plans to give parents a true picture of children's lives.

B   Schools to be responsible for the safety, enjoyment and happiness of children.

C   Social issues in schools will be easier to identify.

D   Schools will be accountable for solving social problems.

E   Plans will reduce teenage pregnancy rates and drug use.

Example question: answer and rationale

A **conclusion** is simply a statement that is logical, that is a proposition arrived at after consideration of the evidence, arguments or premises. This requires you to examine each of the statements and determine which one best provides a conclusion of the passage. The highlighted statement and rationale is correct.

A   **Plans to give parents a true picture of children's lives.**

This is the correct answer as it provides the one best conclusion of the passage. It is stated in the passage that 'report is widely used by parents to find out more about their child's school or when selecting a school in their area.'

B   **Schools to be responsible for the safety, enjoyment and happiness of children.**

This is an incorrect answer as the passage states that 'schools would become broadly responsible' as opposed to the statement itself that suggests total responsibility.

C   **Social issues in schools will be easier to identify.**

This is an incorrect answer as nowhere in the passage does it suggest that it will be easier to identify social issues as this may be determined by the willingness or otherwise of pupils to provide the information required by the targets.

D   **Schools will be accountable for solving social problems.**

This is an incorrect answer even though it is suggested that schools may collect information identifying the social problems of their pupils it cannot be concluded that the schools will be accountable for these problems.

E   **Plans will reduce teenage pregnancy rates and drug use.**

This is an incorrect answer even though schools may identify the incidence of teenage pregnancies and drug use the plans are not designed to reduce these although this could conceivably be a by-product.

3. Identifying an assumption

Example question

The demand for octopus meat is becoming widespread across the retail food industry and conservationists are concerned many species of octopus could be extinct within 10 years. The calls from conservationists for octopus meat to be taken off the menu in restaurants and gastro pubs, and a boycott by high street stores, are being ignored. The promotion of octopus meat dishes by celebrity chefs is also flying in the face of conservation. It is believed that 30% of octopus meat caught within European waters is exported to Far East markets.

Which one of the following statements can be **assumed** from the passage?

A   Octopus are only hunted for their meat.

B   Celebrity chefs are not concerned with conservation.

C   A ban on octopus meat in restaurants would protect some species.

D   The Far East are the biggest consumers of octopus meat.

E   Consumer demand is directly related to advertising.

Example question: answer and rationale

An **assumption** is a proposition that is taken for granted, that is, as if it were known to be true. It is a statement that can be surmised or postulated given the overall context of the passage. This question is asking you to identify which statement can be surmised or postulated from the passage. In identifying an **assumption** the correct statement will not actually be stated in the passage so it is for you to determine the main argument and look for the reasoning to support this conclusion. You need to read the passage carefully to identify the overall argument and determine which one option best answers the question posed. The highlighted statement and rationale is correct.

A   Octopus are only hunted for their meat.

This is an incorrect answer as the passage only deals with octopus in relation to their meat for human consumption whereas the meat or other parts of the octopus may be used for other purposes.

B   Celebrity chefs are not concerned with conservation.

This is an incorrect answer as although the passage states, 'The promotion of octopus meat dishes by celebrity chefs . . .', it does not follow that such chefs are unconcerned about the conservation of octopuses.

C   A ban on octopus meat in restaurants would protect some species.

This is an incorrect answer as it cannot be determined whether or not a ban on octopus meat would protect some species.

D   The Far East are the biggest consumers of octopus meat.

This is an incorrect answer as although the passage states that, '30% of octopus meat caught within European waters is exported to Far East markets', there is no information about the export of octopus meat caught in non-European waters.

E   Consumer demand is directly related to advertising.

This is the correct answer as although the word 'advertising' is not used in the passage it can be assumed from a number of the statements. Octopus meat is advertised by being on the menu in restaurants and gastro pubs, being on sale in high street stores and included in recipes by celebrity chefs.

4. Assessing the impact of additional evidence

Example question
There are about 2 million grey squirrels in the UK, compared to 150,000 red squirrels, the majority of which are in Scotland. Black squirrels, a genetic mutation of the grey squirrel, are also expanding rapidly and there are already about 25,000 in the eastern counties of England alone. The black squirrel was first spotted in the early part of the 20th Century, and they are known to be more aggressive than their grey and red counterparts. What this indicates is that the black squirrel population may well overtake that of the red squirrels and eventually that of the grey squirrels.

Which one of the following statements, if true, would most weaken the above argument?

A   Farmers have no hesitation in shooting squirrels, considering them to be a pest.

B   The population of squirrels generally has increased due to householders feeding them.

C   English Nature has undertaken several initiatives to increase the number of red squirrels in England.

D   Research in the USA has found that squirrel mutations peak and decrease after 100 years.

E   The Woodlands Trust disputes the published figures.

Example question: answer and rationale
In assessing the impact of additional evidence you are looking for which statement would *weaken* the argument of the passage. So you first need to determine what the argument is and then consider the effect of each statement on the conclusion. The highlighted statement and rationale is correct.

A   Farmers have no hesitation in shooting squirrels, considering them to be a pest.

This is an incorrect answer as it does not *weaken* or impact on the argument contained within the passage.

B   The population of squirrels generally has increased due to householders feeding them.

This is an incorrect answer as it does not *weaken* or impact on the argument contained within the passage.

C   English Nature has undertaken several initiatives to increase the number of red squirrels in England.

This is an incorrect answer as it does not *weaken* or impact on the argument contained within the passage.

D   Research in the USA has found that squirrel mutations peak and decrease after 100 years.

This is the correct answer as the passage, apart from providing certain figures in relation to the population of grey, red and black squirrels, also states that the black squirrel population is increasing considerably due in part to its aggressive behaviour. This answer suggests that as the black squirrel is a mutation of the grey squirrel its population will peak within the next few years and then decrease. This is contrary to the thrust of the passage of an increasing black squirrel population.

E   The Woodlands Trust disputes the published figures.

This is an incorrect answer as it does not *weaken* or impact on the argument contained within the passage.

5. Detecting reasoning errors

Example question
In 1953 the European Convention for the Protection of Human Rights and Fundamental Freedoms gave full legal protection, for those countries making up the Council of Europe, to the most fundamental rights and freedoms necessary in democratic societies. The Convention was drawn up when countries were coming to terms with the total disregard from human rights and freedoms in the wake of the Second World War. Since being adopted by the majority of countries throughout Europe, the Convention is now part of international law and individuals can seek help from the European Court of Human Rights where their civil liberties have been violated by the state. However, few practical remedies are available even where an applicant is successful.

Which one of the following statements contains a **flaw** in its argument?

A   The European Convention applies to most of Europe.

B   The Convention was implemented over half a century ago.

C   War breaches human rights.

D   Violations of human rights cannot always be remedied through the Court.

E   Freedom is a democratic right.

Sample question: answer and rationale

Reasoning is the mental (cognitive) process of looking for reasons for beliefs, conclusions, actions or feelings. The questions will normally ask you to determine the **flaw** in an argument so you are looking for which statement does not follow from reasons given for the conclusion. The highlighted statement and rationale is correct.

A   The European Convention applies to most of Europe.

This is an incorrect answer as it is directly stated in the passage that the Convention has been 'adopted by the majority of countries throughout Europe'.

B   The Convention was implemented over half a century ago.

This is an incorrect answer as it is directly stated in the passage that, 'In 1953 the European Convention for the Protection of Human Rights and Fundamental Freedoms gave full legal protection . . .'.

C   War breaches human rights.

This is the correct answer as it cannot be inferred from the information in the passage. It could be made as an assertion generally, given the reference to some of the breaches made in the wake of the Second World War, but there is no evidence in the passage to support this general claim.

D   Violations of human rights cannot always be remedied through the Court.

This is an incorrect answer as it is directly stated in the passage that, 'However, few practical remedies are available even where an applicant is successful'.

E   Freedom is a democratic right.

This is an incorrect answer as it is directly stated in the passage, 'fundamental rights and freedoms necessary in democratic societies'.

6. Matching argument

Example question

Peter seems to have lost a lot of weight over the last 3 months. He must have found a good diet or cut down on his alcohol consumption. I know he is still a heavy drinker so it must be his new diet.

Which one of the following most closely parallels the reasoning used in the above argument?

A   Anyone who smokes cigarettes must be unhealthy. Lillian smokes at least 20 cigarettes a day so she must be pretty unfit.

B   I sent an urgent email to a colleague at another branch but she has not responded. I know she's been working in Holland so she must still be away. She always responds promptly to emails.

C   Giving up smoking is very difficult when you first stop but after 2 months the craving for nicotine eases. Brian stopped smoking 6 weeks ago so the craving should be getting easier for him.

D   Laura wants to keep slim and healthy and knows she must be careful what she eats and drinks. Because she wants to keep slim and healthy she eats carefully and does not drink alcohol.

E   Kul runs 5 kilometres every weekday and 10 kilometres on Saturday mornings. People who regularly exercise should be fit and healthy. Kul should be fit and healthy.

Example question: answer and rationale

In a **matching argument** type question you are looking for a similarity in the structure or pattern of the argument that is reproduced in the correct statement.

In relation to the passage above, we can look for a structure to see if statements have been repeated and which could be represented with the letters X or Y. Note that such statements may not be exactly the same. Two such statements that are contained in the passage are: 'Peter is on a good diet', represented by X, and 'Peter has cut down on his alcohol consumption', represented by Y. Either X is true or Y is true. Y cannot be true, so X must be true. The highlighted statement and rationale is correct.

A   **Anyone who smokes cigarettes must be unhealthy. Lillian smokes at least 20 cigarettes a day so she must be pretty unfit.**

This is an incorrect answer as the passage has a different structure. All people who do X are Y, i.e. Lillian does X (smokes cigarettes) and therefore Lillian is Y (unhealthy).

B   I sent an urgent email to a colleague at another branch but she has not responded. I know she's been working in Holland so she must still be away. She always responds promptly to emails.

This is the correct answer as the passage has the same structure. Two statements that are repeated in a slightly different way in the passage are: 'my colleague must be away', represented by X, and 'she always responds promptly to email', represented by Y. Either X is true or Y is true. Y cannot be true, so X must be true.

C   Giving up smoking is very difficult when you first stop but after 2 months the craving for nicotine eases. Brian stopped smoking 6 weeks ago so the craving for nicotine is getting less and less.

This is an incorrect answer as the passage has a different structure. Most people who do X, succeed in Y i.e. Brian has done X (stopped smoking for 6 weeks) and will succeed in Y (craving for nicotine is getting less and less).

D   Laura wants to keep slim and healthy and knows she must be careful what she eats and drinks. Because she wants to keep slim and healthy she eats carefully and does not drink alcohol.

This is an incorrect answer as the passage has a different structure. If Laura wants X, she has to do Y, i.e. if Laura wants X (to keep slim and healthy), she has to do Y (eat carefully and drink no alcohol).

E   Kul runs 5 kilometres every weekday and 10 kilometres on Saturday mornings. People who regularly exercise should usually be fit and healthy. Kul should be fit and healthy.

This is an incorrect answer as the passage has a different structure. People who do X are usually Y, i.e. Kul does X (regular exercise) and so he should be Y (fit and healthy).

7. Applying principles

Example question
People who participate in high risk sporting activities such as mountaineering or rock climbing know the possible consequences of their sport and should be required to have insurance to indemnify them against the costs incurred when an accident occurs. This indemnity can be used to cover the considerable cost to the emergency services, such as mountain rescue teams and RAF rescue helicopters. Those not insured should be sued for the retrieval of the costs.

Which one of the following best illustrates the principle underlying the argument in the passage?

A   People who have accidents in speedboats should be asked to make a voluntary contribution where they use the services of the Royal National Lifeboat Institute (RNLI).

B   Health treatment, whether arising from everyday life activities or from some form of addiction, should be provided without cost to any individual.

C   People who do not pay income tax or national insurance should not benefit from state subsidies.

D   Private medical insurance is the antithesis of the NHS, undermining a fair and equitable health service for the benefit of all.

E   Road tax and insurance should equally apply to cyclists as it does to drivers of motorised vehicles.

Sample question: answer and rationale

Generally, **principle** means a standard or rule of personal conduct or a set of such moral rules. The passage will contain a particular principle usually in the form of a general recommendation and this will be reproduced in the correct statement.

The conclusion from the above passage is that people who participate in high risk sporting activities should have insurance to indemnify them in relation to any costs incurred when use is made of emergency services. This reasoning relies on the principle that if you take part in high risk activities you should pay for the services required in an emergency. The highlighted statement and rationale is correct.

A   People who have accidents in speedboats should be asked to make a voluntary contribution where they use the services of the Royal National Lifeboat Institute (RNLI).

This is an incorrect answer as it does not suggest that people in speedboats have insurance indemnity to cover the costs incurred by the RNLI.

B   Health treatment, whether arising from everyday life activities or from some form of addiction, should be provided without cost to any individual.

This is an incorrect answer as it does not apply to the principle of the main passage but recommends health treatment is free irrespective of a person's lifestyle.

C   People who do not pay income tax or national insurance should not benefit from state subsidies.

This is an incorrect answer as it does not apply to the principle of the main passage but recommends no state benefits for those who do not contribute tax or national insurance.

D   Private medical insurance is the antithesis of the NHS undermining a fair and equitable health service for the benefit of all.

This is an incorrect answer as it does not apply to the principle of the main passage but suggests that private medical insurance is basically inequitable.

E   Road tax and insurance should equally apply to cyclists as it does to drivers of motorised vehicle.

This is the correct answer as it applies the principle to cyclists as it does to those taking part in high risk sporting activities, i.e. insurance indemnity in the event of accidents.

Chapter 4
Thinking Skills Assessment practice test

14. Introduction

You will be presented with a question paper, either pencil/paper or online, and will be allowed 90 minutes to complete the test. There are a total of 50 questions, 25 problem solving and 25 critical thinking, and these two types of question will be mixed throughout the paper.

When you get the question paper read the instructions carefully to refresh your memory of what is required.

In the assessment itself you are not permitted to use a calculator but may use a dictionary (book or electronic). Any rough working would be done either in the test booklet or, if online, on the area indicated in the instructions.

The following practice questions replicate those used in the Thinking Skills Assessment, but it is a decision for you to make whether you time constrain their completion to the 90 minutes.

Before completing this section it might be useful to refresh your memory as to the two suggested strategies often used in answering these types of questions. The strategies can be found on page 13. Try using both strategies for different questions and see which one suits you best.

The assessment is not a test of knowledge but of fundamental intellectual skills. Do not use your own knowledge of a particular issue when answering any of the questions.

Remember each question has a possible choice of five answers and only ONE answer is correct.

The correct answer to each of the questions is produced at the end of the section. The next section then examines the rationale for both the correct and incorrect answers.

There is also a demonstration test available on the Cambridge Assessment website which you might consider completing after undertaking the practice test and checking the answers and rationale for each question.

15. Thinking Skills Assessment: practice test

1   Thousands of homes are burgled every year in the UK. Only a small percentage of homes are alarmed. If more homes were alarmed the number of burglaries would significantly reduce.

Which one of the following statements best represents the flaw in this argument?

A   It overlooks the possibility that alarms can be deactivated.

B   It assumes having an alarm will deter burglars.

C   It implies that there is a relationship between burglaries and the lack of an alarm.

D   It ignores the fact that there are other deterrents available.

E   It ignores the fact that millions of households are never burgled.

2   The table below shows the percentage of males and females by area of employment within the professional services sector.

Professional Services Sector		
Male	Area of Employment	Female
29.7	Training, Business and Recruitment Consultants	35.8
24.5	Construction Professionals and Property Consultants	8.2
17.8	Legal Services and Solicitors	15.9
13.7	Banking, Finance and Accountancy	12.7
8.9	Media and Marketing	22.1
5.4	Insurance	5.3

The difference between the percentage of women and men employed in Legal Services and Solicitors, Media and Marketing and Insurance is:

A   12.1

B   −2.9

C   6.1

D   11.2

E   75.4

3   J & B Engineering Limited undertook a validation study in order to determine the relationship between their recruitment tests and job performance (JP). The approximate overlaps of the tests with JP are as follows: numerical (N) 50%; verbal (V) 20%; Abstract (A) 33%. V and N also overlap with each other by 15% and V and N overlap with A by 33%.

Which one of the following Venn diagrams depicts this information?

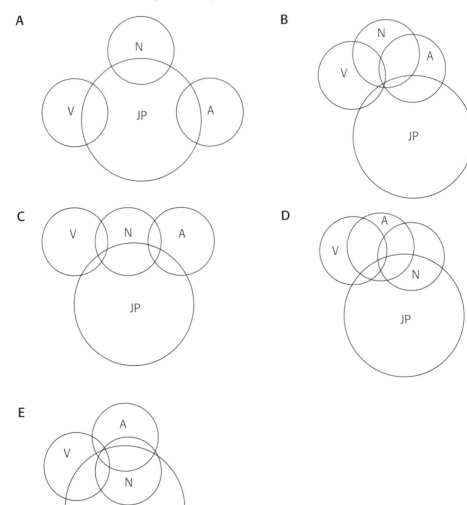

4   We all have to pay for a television licence (barring concessions) even if we never watch the BBC and only watch the commercial channels. You could use your TV just to watch DVDs or videos; or you could just watch ITV or Satellite channels but you will still have to pay the same as someone who only watches the BBC. This system is not equitable and should be changed.

Which one of the following statements is based on a similar principle to the TV licence argument?

A   People with high incomes should not receive child benefit.

B   Frequent travellers using bus, train or plane should pay less than occasional travellers.

C   People who earn more should subsidise those who earn less so that they can afford private health care.

D   Road tax is unfair for someone who has low mileage and we should be charged road tax on mileage bandings.

E   Free bus passes should be means tested.

5   Magic Books Ltd publishes a range of children's books. Their books range from short to long text and they always have an illustration on the centre fold. The books range in size from 16 pages upwards but they are always in multiples of 16 pages, e.g. 16, 32, 48, 64 . . . Page one of the book is always the front cover.

The illustration on the centre fold could have which one of the following page numbering?

A   23 and 24

B   64 and 65

C   14 and 15

D   63 and 64

E   79 and 80

6   The number of people achieving high grades at A-Level has been increasing yearly. Some universities have now introduced entrance exams as they believe A-Level results are not adequately discriminating between applicants. With no evidence of increased IQ it could be concluded that A-Levels have become easier or that pass levels have been reduced.

Which one of the following statements is an underlying assumption of the above argument?

    A   A-Levels are a good predictor of future work performance.

    B   Any results are prone to fluctuation.

    C   A-Levels are no longer valid.

    D   A-Levels have got easier.

    E   University entrance exams will succeed where A-Levels have failed.

7   Bryony has decided to buy a mobile phone from 'Findaphone' on their 'Pay as u Call' option. Bryony estimates that she will use 5 minutes peak rate and 10 minutes off-peak rate in 'phone calls per day. The table below displays the tariff:

Findaphone: Pay As U Call

Cost of phone £49.99			
Cost of calls per minute	£5 voucher	£10 voucher	£50 voucher
Peak rate	40p	35p	25p
Off-peak rate	10p	5p	2p

    How much will it cost Bryony in calls for one month (30 days), ignoring the cost of the phone, if she buys £10 vouchers?

    A   £43.50

    B   £52.50

    C   £57.50

    D   £67.50

    E   £90.00

8   Most police forces operate what they call a 3, 2, 2 system of shift working. Their shift pattern is usually nights 10 pm to 6am, days 6 am to 2 pm, and afternoons 2 pm to 10 pm. Generally officers work 7 days on and 2 days off following this shift rotation. The sleep and eating patterns of police officers are often disrupted and some have difficulty sleeping and eating.

    Which one of the following statements could be assumed from the above paragraph?

    A   Changes to routines may have physical consequences.

    B   Being a police officer causes a loss of sleep.

    C   Shift working causes a loss of appetite.

    D   Working days is better than working nights.

    E   The shift pattern is incorrect and should be restructured.

9 Chat Phone and Easycom contract mobile phones on the following basis: the Chat Phone contract is £30 per month and includes 100 inclusive minutes; additional minutes are charged at 5p per minute. The Easycom contract is £35 per month and charges 2½p per minute.

How many minutes would you have to use for the cost to be the same with both companies?

A 200

B 450

C 350

D 400

E 300

10 The aeroplane has opened up worldwide travel possibilities to millions of people. It used to be the mode of transport of the jet-setting rich but the availability of cut-price flights has made flying a relatively cheap option for all. The level of pollution from aircraft has also naturally risen and individuals who fly regularly significantly increase their 'carbon footprint'. Air travel is now a major contributor to global warming and must be regulated to prevent further damage to the worldwide climate. To ignore the warnings will be detrimental to the survival of Earth as we know it.

Which one of the following statements best summarises the main conclusion of the above argument?

A The world is likely to end due to air travel.

B A ban on planes would reduce pollution.

C The problem of aircraft emissions and the number of flights needs to be resolved.

D Aircraft flights cause changes to the world climate.

E Cut-price flights and the increasing number of airlines are to blame for global warming.

11 Business partners Mary and Hannah are setting up a new dating agency. They want their reception front to be fully glass plated and to maximise their promotion they require an agency name that will read the same vertically when viewed from inside or outside.

Which one of the following names would suit their requirements?

A ITEM

B MATCH

C MAIT

D MOOD

E TEEM

12 During a general election all British citizens aged 18 and over are eligible to vote. The choice of candidate, political party and the strength of the campaign will influence the voter. However, they do have the choice of whether or not to vote. The candidate with the most votes in each constituency will win that seat. The political party with the majority of seats will form the next government. Therefore, the new party will have the support of the majority of the eligible voting public.

Which one of the following statements best identifies the flaw in the above argument?

A Campaigners can influence the voting patterns of the British public.

B Elected candidates could resign whichever way the vote goes.

C A high percentage of the public do not vote and we can never be sure what impact their votes would have on the result.

D The system of voting in Britain is unfair and we should change to a system of proportional representation.

E Voters can change their minds regularly and therefore results are not predictable.

13 Sarah has 3 children aged 8, 4 and 2 years. They all like to eat biscuits. The eldest child likes Shortbread, the middle child likes Chocolate Digestives and the youngest is only allowed Rich Tea. Sarah is very health conscious and limits her children's fat intake on a daily basis. She allows the two eldest children more fat than the youngest but likes to limit the total fat intake for all her children to 4 g per day but allowing the same weight of biscuits each. Below are two tables of biscuits Sarah uses to monitor the fat content:

FAT CONTENT PER 100 GRAMS

Digestive	4.2	Shortbread	4.5
Jammy Dodgers	3.0	Morning Coffee	2.0
Custard Creams	0.9	Hobnobs	5.0
Bourbons	1.0	Ginger Nuts	2.0
Chocolate Digestive	4.5	Oat Crunch	3.9
Figs	1.0	Chocolate Fingers	2.6
Malted Milk	2.1	Jaffa Cakes	0.9
Nice	2.0	Honey Nuts	4.2
Rich Tea	3.0	Arrow Root	2.1
Garibaldi	1.0		

Number of brands by fat bandings

Very low fat (0 – 1 g)	5
Low fat (1.1 – 2 g)	3
Medium (2.1 – 3 g)	5
High fat (3.1 – 4 g)	1
Very high fat (4.1 – 5 g)	5

How many grammes of biscuits can each child have to the nearest rounded whole gramme?

A   100 g

B   66 g

C   33 g

D   25 g

E   50 g

14 If Top Ten Ltd does not increase its dividends then attracting new investors will be difficult and this will affect business expansion plans. This, in turn, would restrict the growth of the business and in real terms could result in a decline of the market share. Either shareholders should be better rewarded or the company must shelve its expansion plans.

Which one of the following statements best expresses the conclusion of this argument?

A   Attracting new investors in business is difficult.

B   If dividends are not increased the business may not grow.

C   Shareholders will have to accept small dividends.

D   Top Ten Ltd may close due to a lack of expansion.

E   If dividends are increased the business will have more shareholders.

15 The shaded area below is the plan of an office building, with a scale of 1:500.

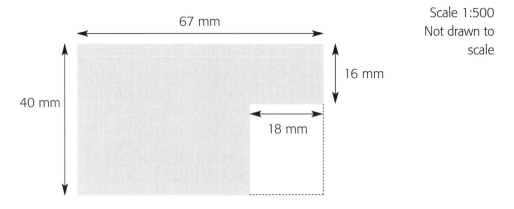

Scale 1:500
Not drawn to
scale

67 mm

16 mm

40 mm

18 mm

What is the actual area, in m², of the office building?

A   562 mm²

B   562 cm²

C   562 m²

D   670 m²

E   670 mm²

16 The level of subscription paid by individuals for private health care does not relate to their level of health. Some individuals pay several times more than others and some pay less but their life expectancies are not significantly different. The suggestion that you receive what you pay for is therefore irrelevant in terms of private health care.

Which one of the following statements is an underlying assumption of the above argument?

A   The cost of private health care is not a measure of its effectiveness.

B   The more you pay the better the health provision.

C   Private health care is no better than the National Health Service.

D   Individuals should be prepared to pay for health care.

E   Life expectancy is a reliable measure of the efficacy of private health care

17 We have two cars in our family in which we tend to do more mileage between April and September. We try to keep the mileages even, therefore, we record the mileages on the first of each month as follows:

	CAR 1	CAR 2
1 April	5,676	5,535
1 May	6,549	6,426
1 June	7,328	7,334
1 July	8,451	8,425
1 August	9,235	9,283
1 September	10,102	10,259

During which month did car 2 do the most mileage?

A   May

B   July

C   August

D   June

E   April

18 There are many mysterious facts about the number 23 and the number 41.

Twenty-three is the lowest prime number with two digits; it has been the subject of two films; Darwin's Origin of Species was published in 1859 (digits add to 23); in the movie *Airport* the bomber sits in seat 23; the digits of the 9/11/2001 attacks add to 23; Michael Jordan and David Beckham have worn number 23 shirts; each parent contributes 23 chromosomes to a child; the Knights Templar had 23 Grand Masters; these are just a few of the facts. Forty-one is the 23rd smallest prime number; it is the atomic number of niobium; it is the number of the last symphony of Mozart; it is a song by the Dave Matthews Band; it represents the 39 lashes Jesus Christ received plus one for the spear in his side and one for the crown of thorns; Charlton Heston's slave number in Ben-Hur was 41; George H W Bush was the 41st President of the USA; 35 mm colour negative film is developed using the C-41 process; again, these are just a few of the facts. Therefore, these numbers are more than numbers that come between 22 and 24 and 40 and 42.

Which one of the following is the best statement of the flaw in the passage above?

A   Any number could be related to a series of facts.

B   The use of these numbers has been chosen in some cases and could be coincidental in others.

C   David Beckham has not always worn a number twenty-three shirt as he used to wear a number seven shirt.

D   The links between some facts and the numbers are very tenuous.

E   Twenty-three and forty-one are not prime numbers.

19 The satellite navigation system in my car rounds all distances up and down on the basis of 0.5 mile to 0.9 mile round up and 0.1 to 0.4 round down. The distance left to travel is shown as 30 miles. The mileometer shows I have travelled another 0.5 mile and the satellite navigation is displaying 29 miles left to the final destination.

Therefore the distance left to travel must now be between:

A   29.9 and 30.0 miles

B   29.5 and 30.0 miles

C   29.2 and 29.4 miles

D   29.4 and 29.5 miles

E   29.5 and 29.6 miles

20 For a documentary on 'The Knife Culture' a survey revealed that up to 5% of the population believe they will become victims of knife crime during the next year; the actual statistic is 0.01%. The fear of 'The Knife Culture' is more predominant with adults even though the group most affected is young males. The internet has been the main media used to access information about knives and knife crime. Whilst some of these sites are developed for valid reasons, some appear to glorify knife crime making it more fearful than it really is. It is time these sites were removed from the internet.

Which one of the following statements, if factual, would reduce the power of the above argument?

A   The internet is too graphic in its portrayal of knife crime.

B   Most people are unaware of the statistics of knife crime.

C   Knife crime has replaced other forms of violent crime.

D   Adults are less likely to access internet sites detailing knife crime.

E   Surveys have accurately identified the population's views on knife crime.

21 Our family all love freshly ground coffee. We also like our coffee to be very strong therefore we add one measure per person and one measure for extra strength. We used to buy one packet of ground coffee every week but now we have a lodger, who also loves ground coffee, therefore we still buy one packet every week but with the addition of another packet every sixth week.

How many were in our family household prior to the arrival of the lodger?

A   6

B   12

C   4

D   5

E   9

22 Some garden centres that specialise in rare plants do not supply mass grown popular plants and prefer to source and cultivate their own range of unusual species. These garden centres do not always attract a large percentage of the general public, as they prefer to plant their gardens with cheaper common plants. Unless these specialist garden centres also supply the cheaper common varieties they are likely to have difficulty sustaining a profitable business.

Which one of the following conclusions best relates to the passage above?

A   Garden centres specialising in rare plants are less profitable.

B   Large garden centres can survive with a rare plant section.

C   The public does not often source rare plants.

D   Garden centres that sell a wide range of products are profitable.

E   Public interest in rare plants is very low.

23 The diagram below shows a round serviette which has three identical segments torn out from around the edge.

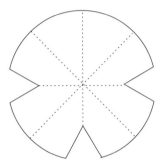

The dotted lines represent the folds of the serviette. Which one of the following diagrams would not be possible once folded along any one of the folds?

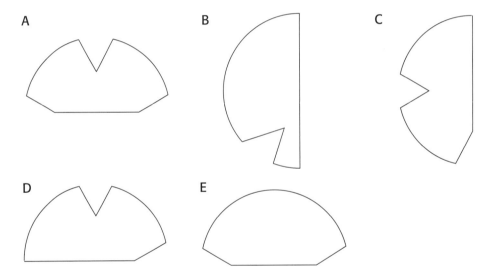

A

B

C

D

E

24 The increase of food centres selling products that are produced locally reduces the cost to the environment and boosts the local economy. It would be preferable to encourage the growth of this business in favour of building more and more supermarkets. Encouraging the public to shop at these centres would reduce the level of wasted packaging, not to mention the wasted transport costs, etc. The land earmarked for future supermarkets could be used to build more local food centres with small food production units which would be more beneficial to everyone.

Which one of the following statements best depicts the main conclusion of the above argument?

A   Food centres reduce the levels of waste.

B   Land can be used for local food businesses.

C   Locally produced food reduces the need for mass produced food.

D   Local food centres are preferable to supermarkets.

E   Small local food centres do not use as many resources as supermarkets.

25   Friends John, Jack and James all enjoy keeping fit. They all arrive at the 'Work Out Centre' at 6.30 pm. John goes off for a squash session, Jack is going to do a gym training circuit and James intends to do a swim package. The schedule for the 'Work Out Centre' is below.

THE WORK OUT CENTRE
Gym and Fitness Club
Arena Leisure Complex
READING

BADMINTON SESSIONS We find you a partner	2 hourly at ¼ past the hour Commencing 11.15 am Duration 70 minutes
PILATES Classes for beginners	2 hourly at 10 past the hour Commencing 4.10 pm Duration 50 minutes
SQUASH SESSIONS We find you a partner	3 hourly at 20 past the hour Commencing 1.20 pm Duration 55 minutes
ULTIMATE SWIM PACKAGE Watersports, swim and sauna	3 hourly at a ¼ to the hour Commencing 12.45 pm Duration 80 minutes
GYM CIRCUIT TRAINING Extensive range of equipment Fully supervised	2 hourly at ½ past the hour Commencing 5.30 pm Duration 65 minutes

John, Jack and James arrange to meet in the snack bar following their sessions. What is the earliest possible time they can meet?

A   9.00 pm

B   8.05 pm

C   8.35 pm

D   8.25 pm

E   8.15 pm

26 As with all drugs the side effects of taking antidepressants can be mild with some and extreme with others. The evidence to support one antidepressant drug over another is non-existent therefore the choice is often made on the basis of the known side effects. The extensive use of SSRIs has come about mainly because they are considered safer than more toxic drugs in terms of overdosing. The press have published disturbing links between suicide and violent behaviour and the use of SSRIs. It has also been claimed that these drugs have great risks when used with other drugs and can have differing side effects with young people. There is a lack of full understanding about how anti-depressants and depression affect the brain. Even the drug companies admit to a lack of understanding about how their drugs work.

Which one of the following conclusions can be drawn from the above passage?

A   SSRIs are safer as a common form of suicide was to overdose on toxic anti-depressants.

B   Using alternative medicine such as St John's Wort is preferable to SSRIs.

C   More extensive research needs to be undertaken by all concerned to extend the understanding of how antidepressants and depression affect the brain.

D   The drugs used to treat depression are no better than placebos and should not be prescribed as freely as they are.

E   The use of 'talking therapies' to treat depression would be more effective and safer than conventional drugs such as SSRIs.

27 The following table shows the marks for a range of subjects using two different tests.

Subject	Test 1	Test 2
History	48	95
Psychology	52	64
English	53	60
Geology	41	69
Chemistry	30	52
Mathematics	80	22

In which other subject was the ratio of Test 1 and Test 2 results similar to that of History?

A   Psychology

B   English

C   Geology

D   Chemistry

E   Mathematics

28 There have been several reported cases of what appear to be unfair judgements made on those who have built unauthorised properties in France and Spain. In some cases this has resulted in the demolition of properties even where local planning permission had been granted. It is a decision that is not taken lightly, but if the national building regulations are ignored in such cases then subsequent cases would have to be treated likewise. No country could allow this to happen, as buildings would be constructed on land designated as 'green' or for other purposes. The national planning and building regulations have to be recognised and adhered to even where local permission has been granted.

Which one of the following statements best illustrates the principal argument of the passage?

A   All unauthorised immigrants must be treated the same according to the laws of the particular country.

B   The sentencing of young offenders for similar crimes may differ due to other extenuating circumstances.

C   Due to health and safety regulations the numbers allowed in a football stadium are restricted.

D   If there is not enough money in the benefit system, then those who have contributed should take priority.

E   Customers in a shop should be served on a 'first come, first served' basis.

29 The following table details the postage rates for different packages by weight.

Format	Weight	1st Class	2nd Class
Letter Up to A5	0 – 100 g	32p	23p
Large Letter Up to A4	0 – 100 g 101 – 250 g 251 – 500 g 501 – 750 g	44p 65p 90p 131p	37p 55p 75p 109p
Packet	0 – 100 g 101 – 250 g 251 – 500 g 501 – 750 g 751 – 1,000 g 1,001 – 1,250 g Each additional 250 g or part thereof	100p 127p 170p 220p 270p 474p +85p	84p 109p 139p 177p 212p N/A N/A

I am posting out 'thank you' cards, which weigh 70 g each, for wedding gifts I received from 12 people. I am enclosing A4 photographs for three people which make a combined weight with the card of 210 g. In addition I am sending two people a 440 g packet containing a card, photographs and wedding cake.

What will be the total first class postage?

A   £6.04

B   £9.34

C   £6.10

D   £5.64

E   £7.59

30 Our insurance company is looking to recruit a sales director who has the confidence to attend conferences where he/she will be required to make promotional presentations. We have short-listed to three applicants but the applicant with the best sales management record has not come out too well on the personality test that we use as an integral part of our recruitment process. The personality test indicates that he is not very

socially bold and that he will probably exert a great deal of nervous energy when placed at the centre of attention. It also suggests that he would not be comfortable in large social gatherings. We have, after consideration, decided not to offer him the post.

Which one of the following statements best highlights the flaw in this argument?

A   The assumption is made that he has no coping strategies for such situations.

B   The assumption is that introverts cannot succeed in sales.

C   Other factors from the recruitment process are not considered.

D   It assumes that the personality test is predictive of behaviour.

E   It assumes that sales directors need to be socially bold.

31 Getaway airport is surrounded by several tall radio masts with warning lights. The lights on the highest masts flash red every 2½ minutes, the medium masts flash blue every 4½ minutes and the lowest masts flash orange every 6 minutes. Periodically they all flash at the same time.

What is the shortest length of the interval between synchronised flashes?

A   90 minutes

B   13 minutes

C   180 minutes

D   30 minutes

E   10 minutes

32 Gordon understands that to become a successful writer he needs to apply his writing skills and that he also needs to put in a considerable amount of work. He also needs to work hard on producing a book that will capture the imagination of the book-buying public. Gordon is determined to write a best seller and he will be working hard to achieve this.

Which one of the following scenarios most closely parallels the reasoning of the above argument?

A   Jennifer really wants to be a very successful actress and has dreams of winning an Oscar. She has just enrolled with RADA and will soon be on her way to her ambition.

B   If you want to be very successful in finance you have to gain experience with large city firms. I do not wish to leave our small town and will have to lower my aims.

C The marriage guidance counsellor is hoping she will be able to reunite the estranged couple. They both really want this and she will talk to both of them at the next session.

D Steven really wants to achieve a first in his geology degree and has to work very hard on his assignments, projects and exam revision. He is confident that his hard work will pay dividends.

E Billy knows that to expand his building business he needs new skills such as plumbing. He has enrolled on an NVQ course in plumbing and will soon be installing bathrooms.

33 The table below shows the daily mileage for the Easy Travel Coach Company.

	Mon	Tue	Wed	Thu	Fri	Sat	Sun
Mileage	2,000	4,000	1,500	2,000	7,250	8,750	5,900

The MD of the company wants the IT office to plot the mileage on a bar chart. The IT office allocate the task to a new member of staff who forgets to insert the detail on each axis and also enters the mileage in a different order.

Which one of the following bar charts is representative of the data?

A
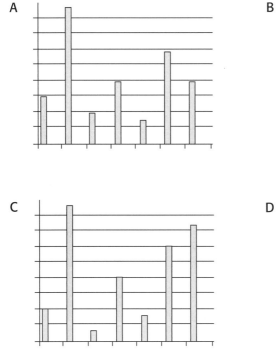

B
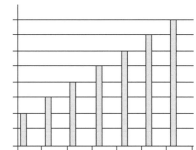

C

D
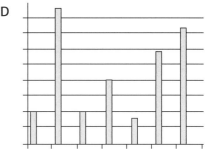

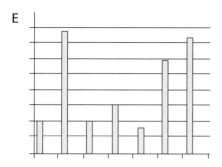

34 The Wildlife Trust has reported that water voles are one of the fastest declining of Britain's mammal species. It is believed that in the last 20 years this species population has decreased by 90%. It is intended to provide protection for water voles' habitats and for the animals themselves. The government is introducing legislation to provide for anyone who kills, injures or disturbs a water vole to be liable to a heavy fine and even imprisonment.

Which one of the following statements is a conclusion which can be drawn from the above passage?

A   Legislation will contribute directly to saving Britain's water voles from extinction.

B   The protection of Britain's mammals is essential in maintaining the balance of nature.

C   The protection of any species is anathema to Darwinian theorists.

D   Preventing the extinction of species is only achievable by regulation.

E   Mammals generally are in decline and their protection is the government's responsibility.

35 The park and ride bus runs Monday to Thursday from 7.30 am to 5.30 pm and from 8.30 am to 6.30 pm on Friday to Sunday. There is no break in this service and each journey lasts 8 minutes. Each bus waits 6 minutes for passengers and at very busy times the wait can be as little as 4 minutes.

In any one day what is the maximum possible number of bus journeys?

A   40

B   50

C   55

D   60

E   75

36 In the global warming debate governments are facing stiff targets on reducing carbon use which has seen the rush to low carbon fuels made from crops. The UK government introduced its Renewable Transport Fuels Obligation requiring that 2.5% of all petrol and diesel is to be made from biofuels, to be increased to 5.75% over two years. However, there is a downside. Land and crops currently used for feeding people will be needed for the production of biofuels. In addition, growing crops requires nitrogen fertilisers and ploughing, harvesting and processing, all of which use energy mostly provided by burning fossil fuels.

Which one of the following statements best expresses the main conclusion of the above argument?

A   5.75% of biofuels used in petrol and diesel will significantly reduce global warming.

B   Using too much land and crops for biofuels will result in food shortages.

C   Biofuels may not necessarily help tackle global warming.

D   Alternative crop production methods are necessary to reduce carbon emissions.

E   The carbon use reduction targets on all countries is obligatory.

37 A round box of chocolates with a diameter of 40 cm and a depth of 3 cm is gift wrapped and tied with a 250 cm length of ribbon which is tied in a bow on top as shown below. After completion of the gift wrapping 60 cm of ribbon was left.

Bottom   Side   Top

A second piece of ribbon also measuring 250 cm is used to decorate a second gift. The ribbon is tied in a similar bow to the first gift and all the ribbon is used.

How many boxes of chocolates are there in the second gift?

A   6

B   10

C   5

D   4

E   12

38 What causes the level of the alternating rise and fall of the seas and oceans known as tides? The answer is, the gravitational pull of the moon and the sun on the rotating earth. It is the gravitational pull of the moon on the earth, which keeps the earth in its monthly orbit and as it is closer to earth than the sun it has twice the effect on the tides.

Which one of the following is the best statement of the flaw in the above argument?

A   It does not take into account the profound effect the weather can have on the tide.

B   It ignores the fact that some areas only have one tide.

C   The assumption made is one of cause and effect.

D   It overlooks spring tides when the lunar and solar tides line up.

E   It ignores the fact that strong winds and abnormal atmospheric pressure makes it impossible to predict tide levels.

39 A game has two bags of balls. Bag 'A' contains four red balls and four blue balls. Bag 'B' contains four red bats and four blue bats.

To play a game you have to have a matching red bat and red ball which are drawn from the bags whilst blindfolded. To achieve this what is the *least* number of bats and balls you must draw from the bags?

A   Five balls and one bat.

B   Three balls and three bats.

C   Four balls and four bats.

D   Five balls and four bats.

E   Five balls and five bats.

40 When one of the leading broadsheet newspapers reported its coup in acquiring Hitler's hidden diaries there was considerable interest both from the literary community and the public at large. The newspaper publisher printed several articles from the diaries before a leading authority proved beyond doubt that the diaries were in fact fakes and had been produced solely for commercial gain.

Which one of the following statements, if true, would most support the above argument?

A   Hitler's diaries captured the imagination of the world press/public.

B   Forgeries of famous people's work are eventually uncovered.

C   The work created by forgers provides a lucrative outcome.

D   Until the diaries were proved to be forgeries they were generally regarded as genuine.

E   The diaries of the infamous will always attract interest and a high price.

41 Below is a table detailing golf buggy hire.

TIGER GOLF CLUB
Summer buggy hire
7 am – 8 pm, 7 days per week

HOURLY RATE	
7 am – 5 pm	£3.50 per hour
5 pm – 8 pm	£2.25 per hour
½ day hire 7 am – 1 pm	£16.00
All day hire	£20.00
Refundable deposit £20.00	

How much will it cost to hire a golf buggy from 2 pm for 5 hours?

A   £17.50

B   £16.00

C   £15.00

D   £20.00

E   £11.25

42 There has recently been considerable 'public outcry' about the cruel conditions in which a large percentage of chickens are reared for human consumption. A celebrity chef has fronted a campaign to educate consumers as to the 'horrors' of battery-reared chickens and encourage them to only buy free-range chickens.

Which one of the statements below is an underlying assumption of the above passage?

A   People who are concerned about animal cruelty do not eat battery-reared chickens.

B   The majority of chefs only use free-range chickens.

C   Free-range chickens are less cruelly treated than battery-reared chickens.

D   All chickens should be treated humanely.

E   Fewer people are buying battery-reared chickens.

43 June is helping her dad pack bait for his pest control business. The bait is in 10g packets. June asks her dad how many packets of bait he needs. Her dad informs her that he sets 20 traps and places 20g of bait in each trap. He works an 8 hour day and he checks all the traps every hour. During the first 5 hours he has to add 10g of bait to half the traps

each hour. During the last 3 hours he has to add 5 g of bait to three-quarters of the traps. If there is a part packet left he adds it to the last trap.

How many packets of bait does June need to pack for her dad?

A   58

B   37.5

C   38

D   57.5

E   60

44 Some commentators would suggest that the spread of sexually transmitted diseases (STDs) has reached almost pandemic proportions, increasing year on year since accurate records were first kept. However, with the exception of AIDS, almost all such diseases are now 'treatable' and have little or no long-term consequences on individual health and well-being. It has been argued that because STDs, apart from AIDS, are of limited risk to health, and their social stigma having lessened over time, public health authorities are failing to meet their obligations in adequately resourcing educational programmes designed to reduce or eliminate STDs.

Which one of the following statements, if true, would detract from the above argument?

A   The number of people contracting STDs will decrease in the future.

B   Providing educational resources for health management is expensive.

C   National Health Service Trusts have increased expenditure on STD educational programmes at the same level as AIDS programmes.

D   The social stigma attached to people who contract STDs will diminish over time.

E   Further scientific advances will reduce the medical interventions required for people with STD's.

45 A cube has sides that each measure 40 cm in length.

What is the volume of the cube?

A   0.064 m

B   0.064 m^2

C   0.16 m^2

D   64000 cm^3

E   1600 cm^2

46 Mortgage lenders have been reducing the amount of funds available for some time. If, as predicted, the recession bites harder then the housing market is likely to be hit even more. As a result first-time buyers will have greater difficulty getting on the property ladder. Therefore, if the recession continues and mortgages become even tighter then first-time house buyers will be badly hit.

Which one of the following statements most closely mirrors the reasoning of the above argument?

A   If the present level of storm and flood damage does not end soon then insurance companies will be inundated with claims. Some insurance companies may struggle to meet the level of claims and payments could take some time. If storm and flood damage become a feature of our climate insurance companies may add extra clauses to policies.

B   If the cost of fuel continues to rise, then people will be more economical and will buy less fuel. The fuel prices will then stop increasing if less fuel is purchased. Therefore, the rise in fuel prices must peak soon.

C   If we do not pay our skilled workers more many of them will seek work abroad. We will then be left with a national skills shortage. Therefore, wages for skilled workers must increase if we wish to maintain a high skills base in this country.

D   If we are all prepared to pay more road tax, then the government could afford to improve the road network. An improved road network would result in shorter more cost effective transport. Therefore, if we want a more efficient road system, we must be prepared to pay higher road tax.

E   The UK car industry has been downsizing for some time. If the industry continues to decrease job losses will be high. Towns and cities whose economies depend on the salaries of car workers would suffer as a consequence. If the decline in the car industry continues then these towns and cities will badly affected.

47 Jane buys biscuits once a fortnight for her grandmother. Her grandmother's favourite biscuits are 96p per packet and she gives Jane enough money for her usual fortnightly supply. At the supermarket there is a multi-buy offer on 10 packets or more. This reduces the packets by 16p each and Jane realises that her grandmother can now have two more packets of biscuits.

How many packets of biscuits does she buy?

A   10

B   12

C   14

D   16

E   20

48 Childhood diseases, such as polio, tuberculosis, diphtheria, etc., which were prevalent up to the middle of the 20th century, are now rare thanks to mass vaccination at an early age. Apart from the significant advances in medical science another important factor in the well-being of children is diet. Food products, such as fresh fruit and a variety of vegetable produce, are now available throughout the year, and not seasonal, as was once the case. Overall this has resulted in better health, not just for children but also into adulthood and old age.

Which one of the following statements best expresses the main premise of the above argument?

A The mortality rate for children should further decrease in the future.

B Eating fresh fruit and vegetables significantly reduces the likelihood of disease.

C Medical science has been responsible for increasing life expectancy.

D There will be a decrease in the rate of illnesses associated with adulthood.

E Availability of food products has been the most important contributor to child mortality levels.

49 I am having friends round this evening for a barbeque. Some of my friends are vegetarian and I can't cook their veggie burgers and veggie sausage with the meat ones. We are due to eat at 7.00 pm and I have drawn up a timed 'To Do' list as follows:

'TO DO' LIST

Make beef burgers and skewer sausages 15 minutes

Barbeque beef burgers and sausages 30 minutes

Cut bread rolls 10 minutes

Make salad dressing 10 minutes

Wash salad 5 minutes

Toss salad in dressing 5 minutes

Make veggie burgers and veggie sausages 30 minutes

Barbeque veggie burgers and veggie sausages 30 minutes

Put veggie food in hot store 5 minutes

Put out patio furniture and lay the table 15 minutes

My barbeque has one grill area and an area for storing hot food. I will serve the food as soon as the meat burgers and sausages are cooked.

What is the latest time I should start preparing the food?

A   5.10 pm

B   5.25 pm

C   5.30 pm

D   4.25 pm

E   5.20 pm

50 Life after death has been a topic of considerable significance not only to the many religions of the world but also at an individual level. No more is this apparent than in the so called 'spirit world', a world populated by 'mediums', those people who purport to communicate between the dead and their living relations and friends. These relations and friends are essentially individuals seeking solace and comfort in their difficult periods of grieving as they attempt to come to terms with their loss. Mediums are probably no less preposterous than fortune-tellers or astrologers, or even the person who reads your future in the tea leaves at the bottom of your cup.

Which one of the following statements is an underlying assumption of the above argument?

A   All religions believe in reincarnation.

B   Mediums can make contact with people who are dead.

C   Those who believe in the spirit world are often relatives of the recently bereaved.

D   Mediums, fortune-tellers and astrologers have extra-sensory perception.

E   Talking to dead loved ones is a comfort to surviving relations and friends.

16. Thinking Skills Assessment: answers and rationale

Below are the correct answers to the 50 multiple-choice questions. A full explanation of the rationale for both the correct and incorrect answers follows in the next section.

Question	Answer	Question	Answer
1	C	26	C
2	D	27	C
3	D	28	A
4	D	29	E
5	B	30	D
6	E	31	A
7	D	32	D
8	A	33	D
9	D	34	A
10	C	35	B
11	C	36	C
12	C	37	A
13	C	38	C
14	B	39	E
15	C	40	D
16	E	41	C
17	D	42	C
18	B	43	A
19	D	44	A
20	D	45	D
21	D	46	E
22	D	47	B
23	A	48	A
24	B	49	B
25	C	50	E

Rationale for correct and incorrect answers

1   This question relates to the passage on page 37.

Which one of the following statements best represents the flaw in this argument?

A   It overlooks the possibility that alarms can be deactivated.

B   It assumes having an alarm will deter burglars.

C   It implies that there is a relationship between burglaries and the lack of an alarm.

D   It ignores the fact that there are other deterrents available.

E   It ignores the fact that millions of households are never burgled.

Question 1: answer and rationale

This question requires that you can identify the **flaw** in the argument presented in the passage. This is an evaluation as to whether or not the options provided best describe the flaw in the argument, in other words are they true or false in relation to the question. In order to address this question it will be necessary to read the passage thoroughly in order to reach a conclusion as to which option would constitute the main flaw in the argument. The options may all appear feasible but you must decide which one option would question the whole premise. The highlighted statement and rationale is correct.

A   It overlooks the possibility that alarms can be deactivated.

This is an incorrect answer as it would not question the whole premise of the argument that there is a relationship between burglaries and whether or not a house is alarmed.

B   It assumes having an alarm will deter burglars.

This is an incorrect answer as it would not question the whole premise of the argument that there is a relationship between burglaries and whether or not a house is alarmed.

C   It implies that there is a relationship between burglaries and the lack of an alarm.

This is the correct answer as there is no evidence presented in the passage as to whether houses that are not alarmed are burgled more frequently than those that are.

D   It ignores the fact that there are other deterrents available.

This is an incorrect answer. Whilst it may be true that other deterrents are available this is irrelevant to the argument presented in the passage.

E   It ignores the fact that millions of households are never burgled.

This is an incorrect answer and is irrelevant as the passage relates only to the number of homes that are burgled.

2   The table below shows the percentage of males and females by area of employment within the professional services sector.

Professional Services Sector		
Male	Area of Employment	Female
29.7	Training, Business and Recruitment Consultants	35.8
24.5	Construction Professionals and Property Consultants	8.2
17.8	Legal Services and Solicitors	15.9
13.7	Banking, Finance and Accountancy	12.7
8.9	Media and Marketing	22.1
5.4	Insurance	5.3

The difference between the percentage of women and men employed in Legal Services and Solicitors, Media and Marketing and Insurance is?

A   12.1

B   −2.9

C   6.1

D   11.2

E   75.4

Question 2: answer and rationale

Multi-stage calculations: rule
This question contains addition and subtraction. The highlighted statement and rationale is correct.

A   12.1

This answer is incorrect as it is the difference between Banking, Finance and Accountancy, Media and Marketing and Insurance, which are not the three sectors the question asks for.

B   −2.9

This answer is incorrect as it is the difference between the two sectors of Legal Services and Solicitors and Banking, Finance and Accountancy, which are not the three sectors the question asks for.

C   6.1

This answer is incorrect as it is the difference between females and males in Training, Business and Recruitment Consultants, which is not what the question asks for.

D   11.2

This answer is correct.

Step 1: add the percentage of females for the three sectors,
15.9 + 22.1 + 5.3 = 43.3.

Step 2: add the percentage of males for the three sectors,
17.8 + 8.9 + 5.4 = 32.1.

Step 3: subtract the total percentage for the three areas for males from the total for females, 43.3 − 32.1 = 11.2.

E   75.4

This answer is incorrect as it is the addition of the percentages for females and males across all three sectors, which is not what the question asks for.

3   J & B Engineering Limited undertook a validation study in order to determine the relationship between their recruitment tests and job performance (JP). The approximate overlaps of the tests with JP are as follows: numerical (N) 50%; verbal (V) 20%; Abstract (A) 33%. V and N also overlap with each other by 15% and V and N overlap with A by 33%.

Which one of the following Venn diagrams depicts this information?

A
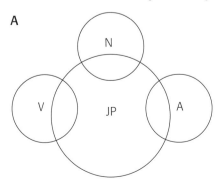

B
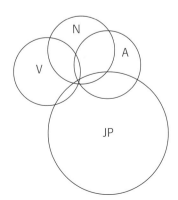

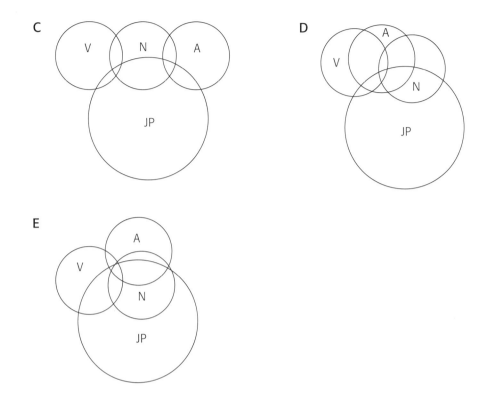

C

D

E

Question 3: answer and rationale

This question requires an examination of the diagrams to identify which can be eliminated immediately. The remaining diagrams then need to be examined closely to check for the right percentages of overlap between the tests themselves and the overlap each has with job performance. Venn diagrams are not always an exact science and you may be looking for the closest match to the data. The highlighted statement and rationale is correct.

A

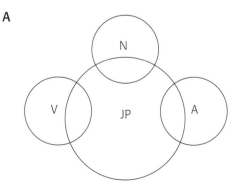

This answer is incorrect and can be dismissed immediately as the question clearly states that there is overlap between the three tests.

B

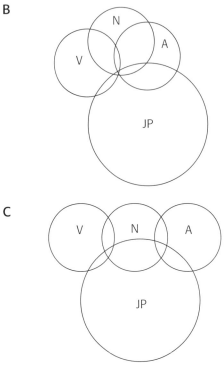

This answer is incorrect and can be dismissed fairly quickly as it is stated in the question that the numerical test (N) has a 50% overlap with job performance which would require the (N) circle to overlap approximately half with JP, which is does not.

C

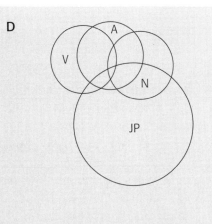

This answer is incorrect but needs more examination before it can be dismissed. The question states that both the Verbal (V) and Numerical (N) tests overlap with the Abstract (A) test by 33% and it can be seen from the diagram that the (V) test has no overlap at all with the (A) test.

D

This answer is correct. The question asks that the numerical test (N) overlaps with JP by 50% and it can be seen in the diagram that the (N) test does overlap roughly 50%. Verbal (V) should overlap with JP 20%, which it roughly does. Abstract (A) should overlap with JP 33%, which it roughly does. V and N should overlap with each other by 15%, which they roughly do. Finally, V and N should both overlap with A by 33%, which they roughly do.

E

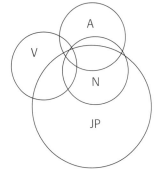

This answer is incorrect and can be dismissed fairly quickly as it is stated in the question that the numerical test (N) has a 50% overlap with job performance which would require the (N) circle to overlap approximately half with JP and it can be seen from the diagram that the overlap is closer to 80%.

4   This question relates to the passage on page 39.

Which one of the following statements is based on a similar principle to the TV licence argument?

A   People with high incomes should not receive child benefit.

B   Frequent travellers using bus, train or plane should pay less than occasional travellers.

C   People who earn more should subsidise those who earn less so that they can afford private health care.

D   Road tax is unfair for someone who has low mileage and we should be charged road tax on mileage bandings.

E   Free bus passes should be means tested.

Question 4: answer and rationale

This question requires that you can identify when similar principles are being applied to two separate arguments. This requires an evaluation of the first argument in order to identify the basic premise. This premise can then be applied to each of the options to identify if there is any similarity. The highlighted statement and rationale is correct.

A   **People with high incomes should not receive child benefit.**

This answer is incorrect as the basic premise of the argument in the passage is that you should only pay proportionately for what you are receiving. The above statement based on this premise could be argued to be the opposite as those on higher income are probably paying more into the benefit system and should perhaps receive more child benefit.

B   **Frequent travellers using bus, train or plane should pay less than occasional travellers.**

This answer is incorrect based on the above premise as frequent travellers are receiving exactly the same as occasional travellers in terms of service. The argument in the passage is not based on how long you watch or don't watch the BBC but on whether you use the service at all.

C   **People who earn more should subsidise those who earn less so that they can afford private health care.**

This answer is incorrect as the basic premise of the argument in the passage is that you should only pay proportionately for what you are receiving. The above statement based on this premise could be argued to be the opposite as those on higher income would be paying more to enable those who are earning less and paying less to receive the same level of private health care.

> D   Road tax is unfair for someone who has low mileage and we should be charged road tax on mileage bandings.
>
> This answer is the correct answer. The road tax system does appear to be inequitable to those who use the road systems less. As a proportion of road tax is spent on maintenance and increases in the network to cope with increased travel it does seem unfair to those who use the networks less.

E   Free bus passes should be means tested.

This answer is incorrect based on the above premise as those with higher incomes and who are potentially paying more into the system would not receive a free bus pass.

5   Magic Books Ltd publishes a range of children's books. Their books range from short to long text and they always have an illustration on the centre fold. The books range in size from 16 pages upwards but they are always in multiples of 16 pages, e.g. 16, 32, 48, 64 . . . Page one of the book is always the front cover.

The illustration on the centre fold could have which one of the following page numbering?

A   23 and 24

B   64 and 65

C   14 and 15

D   63 and 64

E   78 and 79

Question 5: answer and rationale

Book page sequencing: rule
The highlighted statement and rationale is correct.

A   23 and 24

This answer is incorrect and can be dismissed immediately as no matter how many pages there are in the book if the front cover is always counted as 1 then any odd number will be the right hand page of any fold. Therefore the first number of the centre fold has to be an even number.

B   64 and 65

This answer is correct. Firstly, it meets the criteria stated above. The second criterion is that the centre fold will be the middle two numbers of the total number of pages. Therefore, if a book has 16 pages then the centre fold would be pages 8 and 9, leaving seven pages either side. If the book has 32 pages the centre fold would be 16 and 17; 48 pages would be 24 and 25 and so on. Therefore, the left hand page of the centre fold would have to be divisible by 8.

C   14 and 15

This answer is incorrect. It meets the first criteria of an even number on the left hand page but as stated in the example above the left hand page of the centre fold would have to be divisible by 8.

D   63 and 64

This answer is incorrect and can be dismissed immediately as no matter how many pages there are in the book if the front cover is always counted as 1 then any odd number will be the right hand page of any fold. Therefore the first number of the centre fold has to be an even number.

E   78 and 79

This answer is incorrect. It meets the first criteria of an even number on the left hand page but as stated in the example above the left hand page of the centre fold would have to be divisible by 8.

6   This question relates to the passage on page 39.

Which one of the following is an underlying assumption of the above argument?

A   A-Levels are a good predictor of future work performance.

B   Any results are prone to fluctuation.

C   A-Levels are no longer valid.

D   A-Levels have got easier.

E   University entrance exams will succeed where A-Levels have failed.

Question 6: answer and rationale

This question is asking you to determine which statement is an **assumption** made by the writer. An **assumption** is something that is proposed or implied in the passage. An **assumption** may not be expressed in the passage and may not be supported by fact but it should be evident from the overall context of the passage. The highlighted statement and rationale is correct.

A   A-Levels are a good predictor of future work performance.

This is an incorrect answer as no suggestion is made in the passage that A-Level results are predictive of future work performance. The assumption could be made from the passage that they do predict university success.

B   Any results are prone to fluctuation.

This is an incorrect answer. It is explicitly stated in the passage that A-Level grades have been increasing but that is not to assume that any results are prone to fluctuation.

C   A-Levels are no longer valid.

This is an incorrect answer. It is explicitly stated that A-Level results are not adequately discriminating between applicants and that it could be concluded that they are easier or that pass levels have been reduced but this does not assume that they are no longer valid.

D   A-Levels have become easier.

This is an incorrect answer. It is not an assumption but forms part of an explicit comment made in the passage.

E   University entrance exams will succeed where A-Levels have failed.

This is the correct answer. The passage states 'that some universities have now introduced entrance exams as they believe A-Level results are not adequately discriminating between applicants'. Therefore, the assumption made in the argument is that entrance exams will provide the necessary level of discrimination between applicants.

7   Bryony has decided to buy a mobile phone from 'Findaphone' on their 'Pay as u Call' option. Bryony estimates that she will use 5 minutes peak rate and 10 minutes off-peak rate in phone calls per day. The table below displays the tariff:

Findaphone: Pay As U Call

Cost of phone £49.99			
Cost of calls per minute	£5 voucher	£10 voucher	£50 voucher
Peak rate	40p	35p	25p
Off-peak rate	10p	5p	2p

How much will it cost Bryony in calls for one month (30 days), ignoring the cost of the phone, if she buys £10 vouchers?

A   £43.50

B   £52.50

C   £57.50

D   £67.50

E   £90.00

Question 7: answer and rationale

Multi-stage calculations: rule
This question contains multiplication and addition.

The highlighted statement and rationale is correct.

A   £43.50

This answer is incorrect. Using approximations we can round the cost per day from £2.25 to £2 per day then the cost per month (30 days) would be £2 × 30 = £60. We know that because we rounded down in our approximations that the actual cost must be greater than £60, therefore this option is incorrect.

B   £52.50

The rationale for option A equally applies to this option.

C   £57.50

The rationale for option A equally applies to this option.

D   £67.50

This is the correct answer.

Step 1: gather all the relevant information required for the calculations. 30 days' use, £10 voucher which charges 35p peak rate and 5p off-peak rate. Bryony uses, per day, 5 minutes peak rate and 10 minutes off-peak rate.

Step 2: calculate the cost used per day so peak rate is 5 × 35p = £1.75 and off-peak is 10 × 5p = 50p.

Step 3: therefore the cost per month (30 days) is (£1.75 + £0.50) × 30 = £67.50.

E   £90.00

Using approximations we can round the cost per day from £2.25 to £3 per day then the cost per month (30 days) would be £3 × 30 = £90. We know that because we rounded up in our approximations that the actual cost must be less than £90 therefore this option is incorrect.

8   This question relates to the passage on page 40.

Which one of the following statements could be assumed from the above paragraph?

A   Changes to routines may have physical consequences.

B   Being a police officer causes a loss of sleep.

C   Shift working causes a loss of appetite.

D   Working days is better than working nights.

E   The shift pattern is incorrect and should be restructured.

Question 8: answer and rationale

This question is asking you to determine which statement is an **assumption** made by the writer. An **assumption** is something that is proposed or implied in the passage. An **assumption** may not be expressed in the passage and may not be supported by fact but it should be evident from the overall context of the passage. The highlighted statement and rationale is correct.

A   **Changes to routines may have physical consequences.**

This is the correct answer as the passage relates to the changing shift patterns of police officers and the possible loss of sleep or disruption to eating. Therefore, it could be assumed that changes to routines may have a physical impact.

B   Being a police officer causes a loss of sleep.

This is an incorrect answer as the assumption cannot be made that all police officers that work shifts will have disrupted sleep patterns, in fact some may feel no impact.

C   Shift working causes a loss of appetite.

This is an incorrect answer as the assumption cannot be made that shift working results in a loss of appetite just because some police officers on shifts experience this.

D   Working days is better than working nights.

This is an incorrect answer as no comparison is made between the different shifts and the assumption could be made that any disruption would apply to all shifts.

E   The shift pattern is incorrect and should be restructured.

This is an incorrect answer as the assumption cannot be made that the problems stated would change even if the shift pattern were restructured.

9   Chat Phone and Easycom contract mobile phones on the following basis: The Chat Phone contract is £30 per month and includes 100 inclusive minutes; additional minutes are charged at 5p per minute. The Easycom contract is £35 per month and charges 2½p per minute.

How many minutes would you have to use for the cost to be the same with both companies?

A   200

B   450

C   350

D   400

E   300

Question 9: answer and rationale

Multi-stage calculations: rule
This question contains multiplication and addition.

The highlighted statement and rationale is correct.

A   200

This answer is incorrect. The Chat Phone contract of £30 per month includes 100 minutes and additional minutes are charged at 5p per minute, therefore 200 minutes would cost £30 + (100 × 5p = £5) = £35. The Easycom contact is £35 per month and charges 2½p per minute, therefore 200 minutes would cost £35 + (200 × 2½p = £5) = £40. The total amounts for 200 minutes differ and this answer is therefore incorrect.

B   450

This answer is incorrect. To dismiss this answer you would have to do the complete calculation, as above, substituting the additional minutes of 100 and 200 with 350 and 450 respectively.

C 350

This answer is incorrect. To dismiss this answer you would have to do the complete calculation, as above, substituting the additional minutes of 100 and 200 with 250 and 350 respectively.

D 400

This answer is correct.

Step 1: gather all the relevant information: Chat Phone contract £30 per month inclusive of 100 minutes with additional minutes at 5p per minute. Easycom contract £35 per month with charges of 2½p per minute.

Step 2: calculate the Chat Phone cost for 400 minutes:
£30 + (300 × 5p = £15) = £45.

Step 3: calculate the Easycom cost for 400 minutes:
£35 + (400 × 2½p = £10) = £45.

Therefore, 400 minutes with each company would cost the same.

E 300

This answer is incorrect. To dismiss this answer you would have to do the complete calculation, as above, substituting the additional minutes of 100 and 200 with 200 and 300 respectively.

10 This question relates to the passage on page 41.

Which one of the following statements best summarises the main conclusion of the above argument?

A   The world is likely to end due to air travel.

B   A ban on planes would reduce pollution.

C   The problem of aircraft emissions and the number of flights needs to be resolved.

D   Aircraft flights cause changes to the world climate.

E   Cut-price flights and the increasing number of airlines are to blame for global warming.

Question 10: answer and rationale

This question requires that you can identify the **main conclusion** of the argument presented in the passage. This is an evaluation as to whether or not the options provided are the main conclusion, in other words are they true or false in relation to the question. In order to address this question it will be necessary to read the passage thoroughly in order to follow the ideas and structure of the argument to reach the main conclusion. The passage may contain several points that are pertinent to the overall argument as they help to build up the body of evidence. The highlighted statement and rationale is correct.

A   The world is likely to end due to air travel.

This is an incorrect answer. The passage states that air travel is a major contributor to global warming and that it may be detrimental to the survival of Earth but it cannot be concluded that it will result in the end of the world.

B   A ban on planes would reduce pollution.

This is an incorrect answer. The passage states that the level of pollution from air travel is high and therefore it could be concluded that a ban on planes would reduce pollution. However, this is not suggested in the passage and is therefore not the main conclusion.

C   The problem of aircraft emissions and the number of flights needs to be resolved.

This is the correct answer as the passage builds an argument based on the increased number of flights and the subsequent increased levels of pollution. The passage states that air travel must be regulated and the obvious conclusion to be drawn is that aircraft emissions and the number flights needs to be resolved to facilitate this.

D   Aircraft flights cause changes to the world climate.

This is an incorrect answer as it is only part of the argument put forward in the passage and purely a contributory factor to the main conclusion.

E   Cut-price flights and the increasing number of airlines are to blame for global warming.

This is an incorrect answer. Cut-price flights and the increasing number of airlines may have added to global warming but they are not the only contributors. This again is only a contributory factor to the main conclusion.

11   Business partners Mary and Hannah are setting up a new dating agency. They want their reception front to be fully glass plated and to maximise their promotion they require an agency name that will read the same vertically when viewed from inside or outside.

Which one of the following names would suit their requirements?

A   ITEM

B   MATCH

C   MAIT

D   MOOD

E   TEEM

Question 11: answer and rationale

This question requires that you can visualise the words written vertically and flipped horizontally to form a mirror image. Answers in this type of question can be rapidly eliminated when they contain letters or diagrams that are not symmetrical, for example, the letters E, C, and D, when viewed as a mirror image would be, Ǝ, Ɔ, and ᗡ, therefore, answers containing these letters can be dismissed. The highlighted statement and rationale is correct.

A   ITEM

This answer is incorrect as it contains the letter 'E' which as a mirror image would be ' Ǝ' when viewed from the other side of the glass plated reception.

B   MATCH

This answer is incorrect as it contains the letter 'C' which as a mirror image would be 'Ɔ' when viewed from the other side of the glass plated reception.

C   MAIT

This answer is correct as it would read the same when viewed vertically from both inside and outside the glass plated reception.

D   MOOD

This answer is incorrect as it contains the letter 'D' which as a mirror image would be ' ᗡ' when viewed from the other side of the glass plated reception.

E   TEEM

This answer is incorrect as it contains the letter 'E' which as a mirror image would be ' Ǝ' when viewed from the other side of the glass plated reception.

12   This question relates to the passage on page 42.

Which one of the following statements best identifies the flaw in the above argument?

A   Campaigners can influence the voting patterns of the British public.

B   Elected candidates could resign whichever way the vote goes.

C   A high percentage of the public do not vote and we can never be sure what impact their votes would have on the result.

D   The system of voting in Britain is unfair and we should change to a system of proportional representation.

E   Voters can change their minds regularly and therefore results are not predictable.

Question 12: answer and rationale

This question requires that you can identify the **flaw** in the argument presented in the passage. This is an evaluation as to whether or not the options provided best describe the flaw in the argument, in other words are they true or false in relation to the question. In order to address this question it will be necessary to read the passage thoroughly in order to reach a conclusion as to which option would constitute the main flaw in the argument. The options may all appear feasible but you must decide which one option would question the whole premise. The highlighted statement and rationale is correct.

A   Campaigners can influence the voting patterns of the British public.

This is an incorrect answer as it is clearly stated in the passage that the strength of the campaign can influence voters.

B   Elected candidates could resign whichever way the vote goes.

This is an incorrect answer. This could be problematic for those who voted for a candidate who resigns but it is not the main flaw in the above argument.

C   A high percentage of the public do not vote and we can never be sure what impact their votes would have on the result.

This is the correct answer as the passage states that 'the new party will have the support of the majority of the eligible voting public' which is incorrect as a high percentage do not vote and therefore the impact of their vote is unknown.

D   The system of voting in Britain is unfair and we should change to a system of proportional representation.

This is an incorrect answer. This statement may be a view supported by some of the voting public but it does not constitute a flaw in the argument put forward in the passage and is therefore irrelevant.

E   Voters can change their minds regularly and therefore results are not predictable.

This is an incorrect answer as the prediction of results is not covered in the passage and is therefore irrelevant.

13 Sarah has 3 children aged 8, 4 and 2 years. They all like to eat biscuits. The eldest child likes Shortbread, the middle child likes Chocolate Digestives and the youngest is only allowed Rich Tea. Sarah is very health conscious and limits her children's fat intake on a daily basis. She allows the two eldest children more fat than the youngest but likes to limit the total fat intake for all her children to 4 g per day but allowing the same weight of biscuits each. Below are two tables of biscuits Sarah uses to monitor the fat content:

FAT CONTENT PER 100 GRAMS

Digestive	4.2	Shortbread	4.5
Jammy Dodgers	3.0	Morning Coffee	2.0
Custard Creams	0.9	Hobnobs	5.0
Bourbons	1.0	Ginger Nuts	2.0
Chocolate Digestive	4.5	Oat Crunch	3.9
Figs	1.0	Chocolate Fingers	2.6
Malted Milk	2.1	Jaffa Cakes	0.9
Nice	2.0	Honey Nuts	4.2
Rich Tea	3.0	Arrow Root	2.1
Garibaldi	1.0		

Number of brands by fat bandings

Very low fat (0 – 1 g)	5
Low fat (1.1 – 2 g)	3
Medium (2.1 – 3 g)	5
High fat (3.1 – 4 g)	1
Very high fat (4.1 – 5 g)	5

How many grammes of biscuits can each child have to the nearest rounded whole gramme?

A   100 g

B   66 g

C   33 g

D   25 g

E   50 g

Question 13: answer and rationale

Interpreting data: rule

When interpreting data, this may involve identifying information presented in some form of pictorial or visual display. This is usually followed by basic calculations.

The highlighted statement and rationale is correct.

A   100 g

This answer is incorrect and can be dismissed fairly quickly as 100 g of each of the three chosen biscuits adds to 12 g of fat which is three times the allowed fat intake of 4 g.

B   66 g

This answer is incorrect and can be dismissed fairly quickly as 66 g of each of the three chosen biscuits adds to 8 g of fat which is twice the allowed fat intake of 4 g.

C   33 g

This answer is correct.

Step 1: gather the relevant information; the second table is irrelevant to the question; identify the fat content of the children's biscuits, Shortbread 4.5 g per 100 g, Chocolate Digestives 4.5 g per 100 g and Rich Tea 3.0 g per 100 g; 2 eldest children allowed more fat but total for all three must be 4 g; each child should have same weight of biscuits.

Step 2: add the fat per 100 g for the three varieties of biscuits, 4.5 g + 4.5 g + 3.0 g = 12 g for 300 g of biscuits.

Step 3: calculate the weight of biscuits for the specified fat level of 4 g, 12 ÷ 3 = 4 g of fat, 300 ÷ 3 = 100 g of biscuits.

Step 4: calculate the weight of biscuits for each child, 100 ÷ 3 = 33.3^r rounded to the nearest whole gram = 33 g.

D   25 g

This answer is incorrect but you would need to carry out the full calculation to dismiss this option.

E   50 g

This answer is incorrect and can be dismissed fairly quickly as 50 g of each of the three chosen biscuits adds to 6 g of fat which is considerably higher than the allowed fat intake of 4 g.

14 This question relates to the passage on page 43.

Which one of the following statements best expresses the conclusion of this argument?

A   Attracting new investors in business is difficult.

B   If dividends are not increased the business may not grow.

C   Shareholders will have to accept small dividends.

D   Top Ten Ltd may close due to a lack of expansion.

E   If dividends are increased the business will have more shareholders.

Question 14: answer and rationale

This question requires that you can identify the **main conclusion** of the argument presented in the passage. This is an evaluation as to whether or not the options provided are the main conclusion, in other words are they true or false in relation to the question. In order to address this question it will be necessary to read the passage thoroughly in order to follow the ideas and structure of the argument to reach the main conclusion. The passage may contain several points that are pertinent to the overall argument as they help to build up the body of evidence. The highlighted statement and rationale is correct.

A   Attracting new investors in business is difficult.

This answer is incorrect and is not a conclusion that can be drawn from the passage.

B   If dividends are not increased the business may not grow.

This answer is correct. The conclusion to be drawn from the passage is that new investors are needed in order for the business to expand. In order to attract new investors dividends need to be increased, therefore, if dividends are not increased the business may not grow.

C   Shareholders will have to accept small dividends.

This answer is incorrect even though it may be true if the business does not increase its dividends. However, the argument is clearly about business expansion and the impact dividends may have on this.

D Top Ten Ltd may close due to a lack of expansion.

This answer is incorrect and is not suggested anywhere in the passage.

E If dividends are increased the business will have more shareholders.

This answer is incorrect even though it is suggested in the passage that an increase in dividends will attract more shareholders. However, the argument is clearly about business expansion and the impact dividends may have on this.

15 The shaded area below is the plan of an office building, with a scale of 1:500.

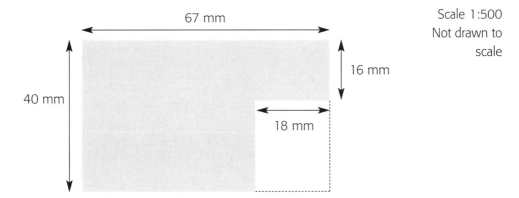

What is the actual area, in m², of the office building?

A   562 mm²

B   562 cm²

C   562 m²

D   670 m²

E   670 mm²

Question 15: answer and rationale

Area: rule
To find the area of a square or rectangle (one-dimensional shape) you multiply the length by the width. As this question contains a scaled drawing you will need to carry out multiplication, division and subtraction.

The highlighted statement and rationale is correct.

A   562 mm²

This answer is incorrect as 562 mm² is a very small area and, according to the question, the answer should be given in m².

B   562 cm^2

This answer is incorrect as 562 cm^2 is a very small area and, according to the question, the answer should be given in m^2.

C   562 m^2

This answer is correct

Step 1: work out the whole area of the rectangle including the dotted lines, remembering to use the scale of 1:500 first and then divide by 1000 to convert the measurements into metres (for ease of calculations).

So $\frac{67 \times 500}{1000}$ = 33.5 m and $\frac{40 \times 500}{1000}$ = 20 m, therefore the area is 33.5 × 20 = 670 m^2.

Step 2: find the area enclosed by the extended dotted lines and take this away from the total area of the rectangle find in Step 1

so $\frac{24 \times 500}{1000}$ = 12 and $\frac{18 \times 500}{1000}$ = 9,

therefore the area of the small area enclosed by the dotted lines is 12 × 9 = 108 m^2.

Step 3: the actual office area is 670 – 108 = 562 m^2.

D   670 m^2

This answer is incorrect; it is the area of the extended area made into a rectangle and needs to have the smaller area taken away from it as in Option C above.

E   670 mm^2

This option is incorrect; it is a very small area and is based on the incorrect area calculated in Option D above. Also, according to the question, the answer should be given in m^2.

16 This question relates to the passage on page 44.

Which one of the following statements is an underlying assumption of the above argument?

   A   The cost of private health care is not a measure of its effectiveness.

   B   The more you pay the better the health provision.

   C   Private health care is no better than the National Health Service.

   D   Individuals should be prepared to pay for health care.

   E   Life expectancy is a reliable measure of the efficacy of private health care.

Question 16: answer and rationale

This question is asking you to determine which statement is an **assumption** made by the writer. An **assumption** is something that is proposed or implied in the passage. An **assumption** may not be expressed in the passage and may not be supported by fact, but it should be evident from the overall context of the passage. The highlighted statement and rationale is correct.

A   The cost of private health care is not a measure of its effectiveness.

This is an incorrect answer as it is explicitly stated in the passage that life expectancies are not significantly different no matter what is paid for health care.

B   The more you pay the better the health provision.

This is an incorrect answer as it is explicitly stated in the passage 'that you receive what you pay for is irrelevant in terms of private health care'.

C   Private health care is no better than the National Health Service.

This is an incorrect answer as the passage does not imply that there is comparison between private health care and National Health Service.

D   Individuals should be prepared to pay for health care.

This is an incorrect answer and is irrelevant in relation to the passage.

E   Life expectancy is a reliable measure of the efficacy of private health care.

This is the correct answer as the assumption behind the argument in the passage is that life expectancy is a reliable measure of the efficacy of private health care, indeed it is the only measure mentioned.

17   We have two cars in our family in which we tend to do more mileage between April and September. We try to keep the mileages even, therefore, we record the mileages on the first of each month as follows:

	CAR 1	CAR 2
1 April	5,676	5,535
1 May	6,549	6,426
1 June	7,328	7,334
1 July	8,451	8,425
1 August	9,235	9,283
1 September	10,102	10,259

During which month did car 2 do the most mileage?

A   May

B   July

C   August

D   June

E   April

Question 17: answer and rationale

Interpretation of data and single-stage calculations: rule

This question requires you to identify the relevant data and then to perform calculations using subtraction.

The highlighted statement and rationale is correct.

A   May

This answer is incorrect as the mileage for May is 908 which is less than the mileage of 1,091 for June.

B   July

This answer is incorrect as the mileage for July is 858 which is less than the mileage of 1,091 for June.

C   August

This answer is incorrect as the mileage for August is 976 which is less than the mileage of 1,091 for June.

D   June

This answer is correct.

Step 1: identify the relevant data, which is the column headed 'Car 2'; the other data is irrelevant to the question. Note, that as the mileages are recorded on the first of each month they are for April to August only.

Step 2: a quick scan of the data should identify that all but one of the differences are less than 1,000. However, you can calculate if you are not confident to do this, see Step 3.

Step 3: subtract the August amount from the September amount to arrive at the total mile for August. Then July from August for July and so on, 10,259 – 9,283 = August 976; 9,283 – 8,425 = July 858; 8,425 – 7,334 = June 1,091; 7,334 – 6,426 = May 908; 6,426 – 5,535 = April 891, therefore, June is the correct answer.

E April

This answer is incorrect as the mileage for April is 891 which is less than the mileage of 1,091 for June.

18 This question relates to the passage on page 45.

Which one of the following is the best statement of the flaw in the passage above?

A Any number could be related to a series of facts.

B The use of these numbers has been chosen in some cases and could be coincidental in others.

C David Beckham has not always worn a number twenty-three shirt as he used to wear a number seven shirt.

D The links between some facts and the numbers are very tenuous.

E Twenty-three and forty-one are not prime numbers.

Question 18: answer and rationale

This question requires that you can identify the **flaw** in the argument presented in the passage. This is an evaluation as to whether or not the options provided best describe the flaw in the argument, in other words are they true or false in relation to the question. In order to address this question it will be necessary to read the passage thoroughly in order to reach a conclusion as to which option would constitute the main flaw in the argument. The options may all appear feasible but you must decide which one option would question the whole premise. The highlighted statement and rationale is correct.

A Any number could be related to a series of facts.

This is an incorrect answer as it would be difficult to associate lengthy numbers to a series of facts and even if true it is not the best example of the flaw in the argument.

B The use of these numbers has been chosen in some cases and could be coincidental in others.

This is the correct answer as it best describes the flaw in the argument. The fact that the two numbers mentioned have, in some instances, been specifically chosen and the possibility of coincidence questions the premise that these are more than numbers.

C   David Beckham has not always worn a number twenty-three shirt as he used to wear a number seven shirt.

This is an incorrect answer as it only poses the flaw in one of the examples given in the passage and not the flaw in the whole argument.

D   The links between some facts and the numbers are very tenuous.

This is an incorrect answer as the suggestion that some of the links are very tenuous does not invalidate the argument.

E   Twenty-three and forty-one are not prime numbers.

This is an incorrect answer as 23 and 41 are prime numbers.

19   The satellite navigation system in my car rounds all distances up and down on the basis of 0.5 mile to 0.9 mile round up and 0.1 to 0.4 round down. The distance left to travel is shown as 30 miles. The mileometer shows I have travelled another 0.5 mile and the satellite navigation is displaying 29 miles left to the final destination.

Therefore the distance left to travel must now be between:

A   29.9 and 30.0 miles

B   29.5 and 30.0 miles

C   29.2 and 29.4 miles

D   29.4 and 29.5 miles

E   29.5 and 29.6 miles

Question 19: answer and rationale

Rounding: rule
Round up if the values are 0.5 to 0.9 and round down if the values are 0.1 to 0.4.

The highlighted statement and rationale is correct.

A   29.9 and 30.0 miles

This answer is incorrect as the final figure from the satellite navigation system is 29 miles therefore this could not have been rounded down from 30 miles.

B   29.5 and 30.0 miles

This answer is incorrect as the final figure from the satellite navigation system is 29 miles therefore this could not have been rounded down from 30 miles.

C   29.2 and 29.4 miles

This answer is incorrect as it is not possible to have a difference of two decimal places.

D   29.4 and 29.5 miles

This answer is correct.

Step 1: extract the relevant information 30.0 miles less 0.5 mile = 29.5 miles. Satellite navigation is displaying 29 miles to destination.

Step 2: the satellite navigation system rounds up or down therefore the distance has to be between 29.4 and 29.5 miles which would account for the rounding process.

E   29.5 and 29.6 miles

This answer is incorrect as the final rounding cannot exceed 29.5.

20 This question relates to the passage on page 46.

Which one of the following statements, if factual, would reduce the power of the above argument?

A   The internet is too graphic in its portrayal of knife crime.

B   Most people are unaware of the statistics of knife crime.

C   Knife crime has replaced other forms of violent crime.

D   Adults are less likely to access internet sites detailing knife crime.

E   Surveys have accurately identified the populations' views on knife crime.

Question 20: answer and rationale

This question requires that you can identify which statement, **if factual**, would reduce the power of the argument presented in the passage. This is an evaluation as to whether the options provided, if they were true, would most weaken the argument. In order to address this question it will be necessary to read the passage thoroughly in order to arrive at the most logical answer. The options may all appear feasible but you must decide which one option would be the most likely. The highlighted statement and rationale is correct.

A   The internet is too graphic in its portrayal of knife crime.

This is an incorrect answer as this statement supports the argument.

B   Most people are unaware of the statistics of knife crime.

This is an incorrect answer. The passage states that those questioned as part of the survey were unaware of the actual statistics of knife crime. This, however, does not reduce the power of the argument for the removal of knife crime information from the internet.

C   Knife crime has replaced other forms of violent crime.

This is an incorrect answer. There is no mention made in the passage about other forms of violent crime and this statement is irrelevant in terms of the question being asked.

D   Adults are less likely to access internet sites detailing knife crime.

This is the correct answer. The passage argues that the main media for information about knives and knife crime is the internet and that these sites make it more fearful than it really is. The passage states that the fear is greater with adults even though the group most affected is young males. It could be realistically argued that the young males are more likely to access these sites than adults, therefore, the heightened fear amongst adults is perhaps generated from other sources than the internet. This would, if factual, reduce the power of the argument presented in the passage.

E   Surveys have accurately identified the population's views on knife crime.

This is an incorrect answer as the passage states that those surveyed over-estimated the likelihood of becoming a victim of knife crime. This may or may not generalise to the population as a whole and even if it does it is irrelevant in terms of the question posed.

21 Our family all love freshly ground coffee. We also like our coffee to be very strong therefore we add one measure per person and one measure for extra strength. We used to buy one packet of ground coffee every week but now we have a lodger, who also loves ground coffee, therefore, we still buy one packet every week but with the addition of another packet every sixth week.

How many were in our family household prior to the arrival of the lodger?

A   6

B   12

C   4

D   5

E   9

Question 21: answer and rationale

Multi-stage calculations: rule

This question contains addition and subtraction.

The highlighted statement and rationale is correct.

A   6

This answer is incorrect. You would arrive at this figure if you forgot to subtract one for the extra measure (which would count as a person).

B   12

This answer is incorrect as the figure is too high and could therefore be dismissed straight away.

C   4

This answer is incorrect and would only be arrived at if the calculation had been made over 5 weeks and either the extra measure or the lodger had not been deducted.

D   5

This answer is correct.

Step 1: gather the relevant information, used to buy one packet per week, addition of one person, now buy two packets every sixth week – therefore now buy seven packets to last six weeks, one measure per person and the extra measure will therefore count as a person.

Step 2: now buy seven packets to last six weeks, subtract one for lodger, one for extras measure (counts as person), $7 - 2 = 5$.

E   9

This answer is incorrect as the figure is too high and could therefore be dismissed straight away.

22 This question relates to the passage on page 47.

Which one of the following conclusions best relates to the passage above?

A   Garden centres specialising in rare plants are less profitable.

B   Large garden centres can survive with a rare plant section.

C   The public does not often source rare plants.

D   Garden centres that sell a wide range of products are profitable.

E   Public interest in rare plants is very low.

Question 22: answer and rationale

This question requires that you can identify the **conclusion** from the arguments presented in the passage. This is an evaluation as to whether the options provided best describe the logical conclusion from the passage, in other words are they true or false in relation to the question. In order to address this question it will be necessary to read the passage thoroughly in order to arrive at which option would be the most logical conclusion. The options may all appear feasible but you must decide which one option would be the best conclusion that could be drawn from all the passages content and not just part of it. The highlighted statement and rationale is correct.

A   Garden centres specialising in rare plants are less profitable.

This is an incorrect answer as this is explicit in the passage and therefore would not be a conclusion which could be drawn from all the information in the passage.

B   Large garden centres can survive with a rare plant section.

This is an incorrect answer. It may be true that large garden centres can survive with a rare plant section but the passage relates to sustaining profitability for specialist garden centres and therefore this is not a valid conclusion.

C   The public does not often source rare plants.

This is an incorrect answer. The passage states that a large percentage of the general public prefer to plant their gardens with cheaper common plants but the conclusion cannot be made that rare plants are not sourced by some members of the public quite frequently.

D   Garden centres that sell a wide range of products are profitable.

This is the correct answer as it is the most logical conclusion which can be drawn from the passage. The passage makes the point that specialist garden centres do not supply the broad range of products which attract a large percentage of customers and that they are likely to be less profitable.

E   Public interest in rare plants is very low.

This is an incorrect answer. The passage states that a large percentage of the general public prefer to plant their gardens with cheaper common plants but the conclusion cannot be made that members of the public are not interested in rare plants.

23 The diagram below shows a round serviette which has three identical segments torn out from around the edge.

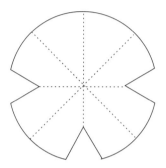

The dotted lines represent the folds of the serviette. Which one of the following diagrams would **not** be possible once folded along any one of the folds?

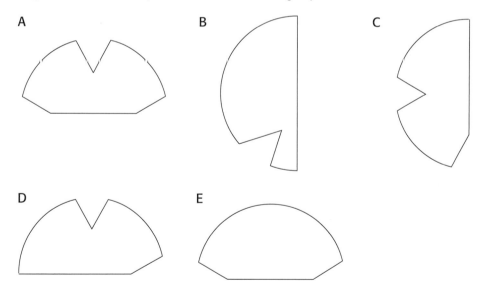

A   B   C

D   E

Question 23: answer and rationale

This question requires that you can use your spatial ability mentally to fold and rotate a shape in order to arrive at the answer. Note the question is asking which shape **cannot** be made. The highlighted statement and rationale is correct.

A

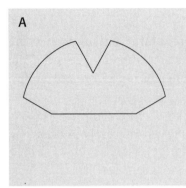

This is the correct answer as this shape cannot be made when the serviette is folded along one of the dotted lines. If the serviette were folded from bottom to top the full curve of the top of the circle would be visible through the segment. If it was folded from top to bottom and rotated 180° the cut out segment at the bottom of the diagram would not be visible. All of the other possible folds are irrelevant.

B

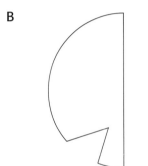

This is an incorrect answer as this shape could be made by folding the shape in the diagram diagonally from bottom right to top left and then rotating the shape 45° round to the right.

C

This is an incorrect answer as this shape could be made by folding the shape in the diagram over from right to left.

D

This is an incorrect answer as this shape could be made by folding the shape in the diagram over from left to right and then rotating the shape 90° to the left.

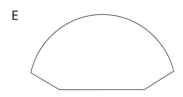

E   This is an incorrect answer as this shape could be made by folding the shape in the diagram from top to bottom and then rotating the shape 180°.

24 This question relates to the passage on page 48.

Which one of the following best depicts the main conclusion of the above argument?

A   Food centres reduce the levels of waste.

B   Land can be used for local food businesses.

C   Locally produced food reduces the need for mass produced food.

D   Local food centres are preferable to supermarkets.

E   Small local food centres do not use as many resources as supermarkets.

Question 24: answer and rationale

This question requires that you can identify the **main conclusion** of the argument presented in the passage. This is an evaluation as to whether or not the options provided are the main conclusion, in other words are they true or false in relation to the question. In order to address this question it will be necessary to read the passage thoroughly in order to follow the ideas and structure of the argument to reach the main conclusion. The passage may contain several points that are pertinent to the overall argument as they help to build up the body of evidence. The highlighted statement and rationale is correct.

A   Food centres reduce the levels of waste.

This is an incorrect answer. The passage does make the point that the wasted packaging is less from food centres as opposed to supermarkets but it only forms part of the main conclusion.

B   Land can be used for local food businesses.

This is the correct answer as the passage builds an argument for the use of available building land being used for local food businesses as opposed to supermarkets due to the benefits to the environment and local economies.

C   Locally produced food reduces the need for mass produced food.

This is an incorrect answer and does not form part of the argument put forward in the passage. It could be assumed that this would be the case but it would be a weak conclusion to draw from the passage.

D   Local food centres are preferable to supermarkets.

This is an incorrect answer even though it is a conclusion which could be drawn from the content of the passage. However, it does not take into account the use of future building land.

E   Small local food centres do not use as many resources as supermarkets.

This is an incorrect answer albeit a part of the argument put forward in the passage. Again, this answer does not take into account the main points of the passage.

25   Friends John, Jack and James all enjoy keeping fit. They all arrive at the 'Work Out Centre' at 6.30 pm. John goes off for a squash session, Jack is going to do a gym circuit and James intends to do a swim package. The schedule for the 'Work Out Centre' is below.

THE WORK OUT CENTRE
Gym and Fitness Club
Arena Leisure Complex
READING

BADMINTON SESSIONS We find you a partner	2 hourly at ¼ past the hour Commencing 11.15 am Duration 70 minutes
PILATES Classes for beginners	2 hourly at 10 past the hour Commencing 4.10 pm Duration 50 minutes
SQUASH SESSIONS We find you a partner	3 hourly at 20 past the hour Commencing 1.20 pm Duration 55 minutes
ULTIMATE SWIM PACKAGE Watersports, swim and sauna	3 hourly at a ¼ to the hour Commencing 12.45 pm Duration 80 minutes
GYM CIRCUIT TRAINING Extensive range of equipment Fully supervised	2 hourly at ¼ past the hour Commencing 5.30 pm Duration 65 minutes

John, Jack and James arrange to meet in the snack bar following their sessions. What is the earliest possible time they can meet?

A   9.00 pm

B   8.05 pm

C   8.35 pm

D   8.25 pm

E   8.15 pm

Question 25: answer and rationale

Extracting information and multi-stage calculations: rule

This question requires that you can extract the relevant information from a table and perform addition.

The highlighted statement and rationale is correct.

A   9.00 pm

This answer is incorrect as it exceeds any of the finishing times.

B   8.05 pm

This answer is incorrect as it is the finishing time for the swim package which is too early for Jack who is doing the gym circuit training.

C   8.35 pm

This answer is correct.

Step 1: extract the relevant information, they all arrive at 6.30 pm, John goes to squash, Jack goes to the gym circuit, James goes to the swim package, what is the earliest possible time to meet after.

Step 2: calculate start and finishing times for all three sessions, squash 3 hourly at 20 past the hour – commencing 1.20 pm – duration 55 minutes, start time 1.20 pm + 3 hours = 4.20 pm (too early) + 3 hours = 7.20 pm – therefore John starts squash at 7.20 pm + duration 55 minutes = 8.15 pm finish time; gym circuit 2 hourly at ½ past the hour – commencing 5.30 pm – duration 65 minutes, start time 5.30 pm + 2 hours = 7.30 pm – therefore Jack starts gym circuit at 7.30 pm + 65 minutes = 8.35 pm finish time; swim package 3 hourly at ¼ to the hour commencing 12.45 pm – duration 80 minutes, start time 12.45 pm + 3 hours 3.45 pm (too early) + 3 hours 6.45 pm – therefore James starts swimming at 6.45 pm + duration 80 minutes = 8.05 pm.

D   8.25 pm

This answer is incorrect and, if arrived at, would indicate an incorrect addition of the times.

E   8.15 pm

This answer is incorrect as it is the finishing time for the squash which is too early for Jack who is doing the gym circuit training.

26 This question relates to the passage on page 50.

Which one of the following conclusions can be drawn from the above passage?

A   SSRIs are safer as a common form of suicide was to overdose on toxic antidepressants.

B   Using alternative medicine such as St John's Wort is preferable to SSRIs.

C   More extensive research needs to be undertaken by all concerned to extend the understanding of how antidepressants and depression affect the brain.

D   The drugs used to treat depression are no better than placebos and should not be prescribed as freely as they are.

E   The use of 'talking therapies' to treat depression would be more effective and safer than conventional drugs such as SSRIs.

Question 26: answer and rationale

This question requires that you can identify the **main conclusion** of the argument presented in the passage. This is an evaluation as to whether or not the options provided are the main conclusion, in other words are they true or false in relation to the question. In order to address this question it will be necessary to read the passage thoroughly in order to follow the ideas and structure of the argument to reach the main conclusion. The passage may contain several points that are pertinent to the overall argument as they help to build up the body of evidence. The highlighted statement and rationale is correct.

A   SSRIs are safer as a common form of suicide was to overdose on toxic antidepressants.

This is an incorrect answer as it is only part of the argument put forward in the passage and therefore would be a poor conclusion.

B   Using alternative medicine such as St John's Wort is preferable to SSRIs.

This is an incorrect answer as alternative medicines are not mentioned in the passage. One could draw this conclusion based on one's own views but it would not be supported by the content of the passage.

C   More extensive research needs to be undertaken by all concerned to extend the understanding of how antidepressants and depression affect the brain.

This is the correct answer as it is the most logical conclusion that could be drawn given the information in the passage. The passage highlights the problematic nature of antidepressants and the lack of understanding all concerned have about their effects.

D   The drugs used to treat depression are no better than placebos and should not be prescribed as freely as they are.

This is an incorrect answer as the use of placebos is not discussed in the passage. Again, one could draw this conclusion based on one's own views but it would not be supported by the content of the passage.

E   The use of 'talking therapies' to treat depression would be more effective and safer than conventional drugs such as SSRIs.

This is an incorrect answer as 'talking therapies' are not detailed in the passage. This conclusion could be drawn from information acquired from other reading but it would not be supported by the content of the passage.

27 The following table shows the marks for a range of subjects using two different tests.

SUBJECT	TEST 1	TEST 2
History	48	95
Psychology	52	64
English	53	60
Geology	41	69
Chemistry	30	52
Mathematics	80	22

In which other subject was the ratio of Test 1 and Test 2 results similar to that of History?

A   Psychology

B   English

C   Geology

D   Chemistry

E   Mathematics

Question 27: answer and rationale

Ratio: rule
This question requires you to compare two results in the form of a ratio and then to identify the most similar ratio to that of History.

The highlighted statement and rationale is correct.

A   Psychology

This answer is incorrect as the ratio of 5:6 is almost even, not 1:2 as required.

B   English

This answer is incorrect as the ratio is the same as Psychology not Geology.

C   Geology

This answer is correct.

Step 1: approximate the ratio of Test 1 and Test 2 for History 48:95 cancelled out is 1:2.

Step 2: approximate the other ratios, Psychology 52:64 is 5:6; English 53:60 cancelled out is 5:6; Geology 41:69 cancelled out is 2:3.5 (which cancelled out to 1:1.75 is the closest to 1:2; Chemistry 30:53 cancelled out is 3:5; Mathematics 80:22 cancelled out is 4:1.

D   Chemistry

This answer is incorrect but you would have to cancel out 3:5 to discount this answer. The result would be 1:1.66 and 1.66 is not as close to 2 as 1.75.

E   Mathematics

This answer is incorrect and could be dismissed immediately as the ratio has the highest value for Test 1.

28   This question relates to the passage on page 51.

Which one of the following statements best illustrates the principal argument of the passage?

   A   All unauthorised immigrants must be treated the same according to the laws of the particular country.

   B   The sentencing of young offenders for similar crimes may differ due to other extenuating circumstances.

C Due to health and safety regulations the numbers allowed in a football stadium are restricted.

D If there is not enough money in the benefit system, then those who have contributed should take priority.

E Customers in a shop should be served on a 'first come, first served' basis.

Question 28: answer and rationale

This question requires that you can identify the principle in the form of a standard or rule of personal conduct or a set of such moral rules. The principle will usually be in the form of a general recommendation reproduced in the correct statement. The highlighted statement and rationale is correct.

A All unauthorised immigrants must be treated the same according to the laws of the particular country.

This is the correct answer as the principle being applied in both the passage and the statement are similar. The basic principle being applied is one of consistency of application according to the national building regulations in the passage and immigration laws in the statement which are both restrictions based on law.

B The sentencing of young offenders for similar crimes may differ due to other extenuating circumstances.

This is an incorrect answer as the principle being applied in this statement is one where the law or rule being applied is different due to other circumstances.

C Due to health and safety regulations the numbers allowed in a football stadium are restricted.

This is an incorrect answer as it applies to the application of a health and safety regulation which is a law applied to protect the public. The law being applied in the passage is restrictive.

D If there is not enough money in the benefit system, then those who have contributed should take priority.

This is an incorrect answer as the benefit system is based on a principle of need which is fair to all and this statement would contradict the rule being applied.

E Customers in a shop should be served on a 'first come, first served' basis.

This is an incorrect answer as the principle being applied is based on a moral code of conduct rather than legally applied rule.

29 The following table details the postage rates for different packages by weight.

Format	Weight	1st Class	2nd Class
Letter Up to A5	0 – 100 g	32p	23p
Large Letter Up to A4	0 – 100 g 101 – 250 g 251 – 500 g 501 – 750 g	44p 65p 90p 131p	37p 55p 75p 109p
Packet	0 – 100 g 101 – 250 g 251 – 500 g 501 – 750 g 751 – 1,000 g 1,001 – 1,250 g Each additional 250 g or part thereof	100p 127p 170p 220p 270p 474p +85p	84p 109p 139p 177p 212p N/A N/A

I am posting out 'thank you' cards, which weigh 70 g each, for wedding gifts I received from 12 people. I am enclosing A4 photographs for three people which make a combined weight with the card of 210 g. In addition I am sending two people a 440 g packet containing a card, photographs and wedding cake.

What will be the total first class postage?

A   £6.04

B   £9.34

C   £6.10

D   £5.64

E   £7.59

Question 29: answer and rationale

Extracting information and multi-stage calculation: rule
This question requires that you can extract the correct information from a table and perform the necessary multiplication and addition.

The highlighted statement and rationale is correct.

A   £6.04

This answer is incorrect as it is the total cost for the same items at the second class postage rate.

B   £9.34

This answer is incorrect as it has used the next weights up in the table for the large letters and packets.

C   £6.10

This answer is incorrect as it has used the next weights down in the table for the large letters and packets.

D   £5.64

This answer is incorrect as it is the total cost for the letters and packets without the large letters.

E   £7.59

This answer is correct.

Step 1: extract the relevant information, 12 items all first class, 3 A4 large letters at 210 g, 2 packets at 440 g, remaining 7 items are letters.

Step 2: look up postage, 7 first class letters weighing 70 g each at 32p each, 3 first class large letters weighing 210 g each at 65p each, 2 first class packets weighing 440 g each at £1.70 each.

Step 3: multiply the values. 7 × .32p = £3.24, 3 × .65p = £1.95, 2 × £1.70 = £3.40.

Step 4: Add the values, £3.24 + £1.95 + £3.40 = £7.59.

30   This question relates to the passage on page 52.

Which one of the following statements best highlights the flaw in this argument?

A   The assumption is made that he has no coping strategies for such situations.

B   The assumption is that introverts cannot succeed in sales.

C   Other factors from the recruitment process are not considered.

D   It assumes that the personality test is predictive of behaviour.

E   It assumes that sales directors need to be socially bold.

Question 30: answer and rationale

This question requires that you can identify the **flaw** in the argument presented in the passage. This is an evaluation as to whether or not the options provided best describe the flaw in the argument, in other words are they true or false in relation to the question. In order to address this question it will be necessary to read the passage thoroughly in order to reach a conclusion as to which option would constitute the main flaw in the argument. The options may all appear feasible but you must decide which one option would question the whole premise. The highlighted statement and rationale is correct.

A   The assumption is made that he has no coping strategies for such situations.

This answer is incorrect. Whilst this option may be feasible it is not the best example of the flaw in the argument.

B   The assumption is that introverts cannot succeed in sales.

This answer is incorrect as it would require a knowledge of the differing traits between extroverts and introverts in order to arrive at this answer.

C   Other factors from the recruitment process are not considered.

This answer is incorrect. Whilst this option may be feasible it is not the best example of the flaw in the argument.

D   It assumes that the personality test is predictive of behaviour.

This is the correct answer as the assumption is made that the personality test used in the recruitment process is predictive of sales performance. As stated in the passage the test provided differing indicators for the candidate with the best sale management record and may not therefore be a valid predictor.

E   It assumes that sales directors need to be socially bold.

This answer is incorrect as it is only one of the issues raised from the personality test which relate to the flaw in the argument.

31 Getaway airport is surrounded by several tall radio masts with warning lights. The lights on the highest masts flash red every 2½ minutes, the medium masts flash blue every 4½ minutes and the lowest masts flash orange every 6 minutes. Periodically they all flash at the same time.

What is the shortest length of the interval between synchronised flashes?

A   90 minutes

B   13 minutes

C   180 minutes

D   30 minutes

E   10 minutes

Question 31: answer and rationale

Division: rule
This question contains division.

The highlighted statement and rationale is correct.

> **A   90 minutes**
>
> This answer is correct.
>
> *Step 1:* the intervals between flashes have to divide equally into the lowest possible number of minutes to arrive at synchronisation, 90 ÷ 2½ minutes = 36 times, 90 ÷ 4½ minutes = 20 times, 90 ÷ 6 minutes = 15 times, therefore 90 minutes is the shortest possible length of time.

B   13 minutes

This answer is incorrect as it cannot be evenly divided by any of the intervals in the question.

C   180 minutes

This answer is incorrect as it is not the shortest interval of time between synchronised flashes.

D   30 minutes

This answer is incorrect as the blue mast which flashes every 4½ minutes would not be synchronised with the other two.

E   10 minutes

This answer is incorrect and can be dismissed immediately as it cannot be divided by two of the intervals.

32 This question relates to the passage on page 53.

Which one of the following scenarios most closely parallels the reasoning of the above argument?

A Jennifer really wants to be a very successful actress and has dreams of winning an Oscar. She has just enrolled with RADA and will soon be on her way to her ambition.

B If you want to be very successful in finance you have to gain experience with large city firms. I do not wish to leave our small town and will have to lower my aims.

C The marriage guidance counsellor is hoping she will be able to reunite the estranged couple. They both really want this and she will talk to both of them at the next session.

D Steven really wants to achieve a first in his geology degree and has to work very hard on his assignments, projects and exam revision. He is confident that his hard work will pay dividends.

E Billy knows that to expand his building business he needs new skills such as plumbing. He has enrolled on an NVQ course in plumbing and will soon be installing bathrooms.

Question 32: answer and rationale

This question requires that you can examine the passage and identify a similarity in the structure or pattern of the argument that is reproduced in the correct statement. The highlighted statement and rationale is correct.

A Jennifer really wants to be a very successful actress and has dreams of winning an Oscar. She has just enrolled with RADA and will soon be on her way to her ambition.

This answer is incorrect as it is based on ideological dreams of success and does not parallel the argument of hard work, etc.

B If you want to be very successful in finance you have to gain experience with large city firms. I do not wish to leave our small town and will have to lower my aims.

This answer is incorrect and if anything is contrary to the argument put forward in the passage.

C The marriage guidance counsellor is hoping she will be able to reunite the estranged couple. They both really want this and she will talk to both of them at the next session.

This answer is incorrect as the hope of success is related to third parties and does not therefore parallel the argument in the passage.

D   Steven really wants to achieve a first in his geology degree and has to work very hard on his assignments, projects and exam revision. He is confident that his hard work will pay dividends.

This answer is correct as it most closely parallels the argument in the passage. The general premise is one of hard work, determination and confidence of personal success.

E   Billy knows that to expand his building business he needs new skills such as plumbing. He has enrolled on an NVQ course in plumbing and will soon be installing bathrooms.

This answer is incorrect as there is no mention of working hard to achieve the stated goals.

33 The table below shows the daily mileage for the Easy Travel Coach Company.

	Mon	Tue	Wed	Thu	Fri	Sat	Sun
Mileage	2,000	4,000	1,500	2,000	7,250	8,750	5,900

The MD of the company wants the IT office to plot the mileage on a bar chart. The IT office allocate the task to a new member of staff who forgets to insert the detail on each axis and also enters the mileage in a different order.

Which one of the following bar charts is representative of the data?

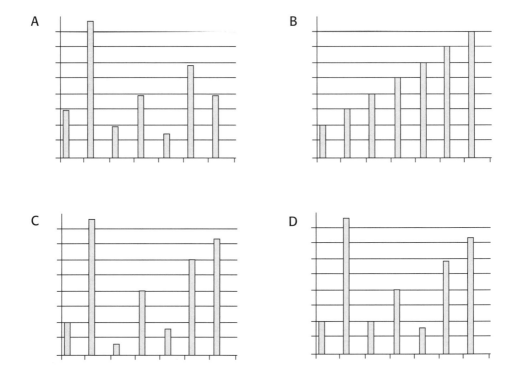

E
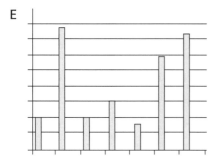

Question 33: answer and rationale

Interpreting data from charts: rule

This question requires that you can logically interpret data presented in bar charts where values are missing.

A
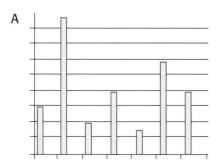

This answer is incorrect as the two values of 2,000 would have to be on an interval scale of 500 to be correct and this would result in a possible maximum of 4,500 on this chart which is too low.

B
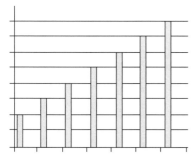

This answer is incorrect and can be dismissed immediately as it does not contain two values the same.

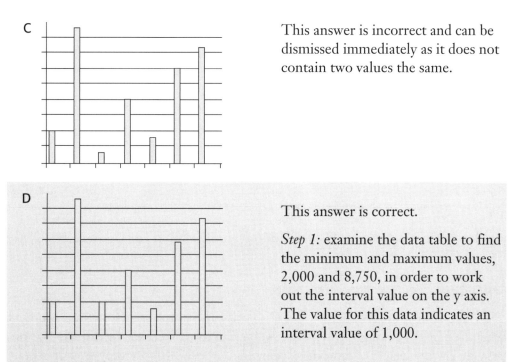

C

This answer is incorrect and can be dismissed immediately as it does not contain two values the same.

D

This answer is correct.

Step 1: examine the data table to find the minimum and maximum values, 2,000 and 8,750, in order to work out the interval value on the y axis. The value for this data indicates an interval value of 1,000.

Step 2: there are two values the same in the data table and therefore check that the chart contains two values of 2,000.

Step 3: check the remaining values.

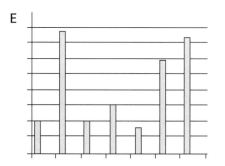

E

This answer is incorrect but would need to be examined carefully before dismissing it. If the two values of 2,000 are correctly displayed then the maximum possible on this chart would be 7,750 which is too low.

34 This question relates to the passage on page 55.

Which one of the following statements is a conclusion which can be drawn from the above passage?

A   Legislation will contribute directly to saving Britain's water voles from extinction.

B   The protection of Britain's mammals is essential in maintaining the balance of nature.

C   The protection of any species is anathema to Darwinian theorists.

D   Preventing the extinction of species is only achievable by regulation.

E   Mammals generally are in decline and their protection is the government's responsibility.

Question 34: answer and rationale

This question requires that you can identify the **conclusion** of the argument presented in the passage. This is an evaluation as to whether or not the options provided a conclusion which can be drawn, in other words are they true or false in relation to the question. In order to address this question it will be necessary to read the passage thoroughly in order to follow that ideas and the structure of the argument to reach the main conclusion. The passage may contain several points that are pertinent to the overall argument as they help to build up the body of evidence. The highlighted statement and rationale is correct.

A   **Legislation will contribute directly to saving Britain's water voles from extinction.**

This is the correct answer as it is explicit from the passage that it is believed that legislation to protect the water vole and its habitats will prevent any further decline in the species and help to reverse the current trend.

B   The protection of Britain's mammals is essential in maintaining the balance of nature.

This answer is incorrect as the passage refers only to one species, the water vole, and does not generalise to mammals per se.

C   The protection of any species is anathema to Darwinian theorists.

This answer is incorrect as it puts forward an argument that is not discussed or even implied in the passage.

D   Preventing the extinction of species is only achievable by regulation.

This answer is incorrect. It could be argued that this is implied in the passage but there is no evidence to support this as being the best conclusion that could be drawn.

E   Mammals generally are in decline and their protection is the government's responsibility.

This answer is incorrect and would be a poor conclusion to draw from the information as it would absolve the public from any responsibility themselves.

35 The park and ride bus runs Monday to Thursday from 7.30 am to 5.30 pm and from 8.30 am to 6.30 pm on Friday to Sunday. There is no break in this service and each journey lasts 8 minutes. Each bus waits 6 minutes for passengers and at very busy times the wait can be as little as 4 minutes.

In any one day what is the maximum possible number of bus journeys?

A   40

B   50

C   55

D   60

E   75

Question 35: answer and rationale

Multi-stage calculations: rule
This question contains addition, division and multiplication.

The highlighted statement and rationale is correct.

A   40

This answer is incorrect and could not be arrived even if the longer wait time of 6 minutes were used.

B   50

This answer is correct.

Step 1: calculate the maximum possible hours in any one day, 7.30am to 5.30 pm = 10 hours, 8.30 am to 6.30 pm = 10 hours.

Step 2: calculate the maximum possible journeys per hour, each journey last 8 minutes and the wait can be as little as 4 minutes, therefore 8 minutes + 4 minutes = 12 minutes, 60 minutes divided by 12 minutes = 5 journeys per hour.

Step 3: calculate the maximum possible journeys in any one day (which will include busy times), $10 \times 5 = 50$.

C 55

This answer is incorrect and would indicate a miscalculation.

D 60

This answer is incorrect and would indicate a miscalculation.

E 75

This answer is incorrect and could only be arrived at if the wait time was not added in.

36 This question relates to the passage on page 56.

Which one of the following statements best expresses the main conclusion of the above argument?

A 5.75% of biofuels used in petrol and diesel will significantly reduce global warming.

B Using too much land and crops for biofuels will result in food shortages.

C Biofuels may not necessarily help tackle global warming.

D Alternative crop production methods are necessary to reduce carbon emissions.

E The carbon use reduction targets on all countries is obligatory.

Question 36: answer and rationale

This question requires that you can identify the **main conclusion** of the argument presented in the passage. This is an evaluation as to whether the options provided are the main conclusion, in other words are they true or false in relation to the question. In order to address this question it will be necessary to read the passage thoroughly in order to follow the ideas and structure of the argument to reach the main conclusion. The passage may contain several points that are pertinent to the overall argument as they help to build up the body of evidence. The highlighted statement and rationale is correct.

A 5.75% of biofuels used in petrol and diesel will significantly reduce global warming.

This answer is incorrect as it is only part of the argument put forward in the passage and cannot therefore be the main conclusion.

B Using too much land and crops for biofuels will result in food shortages.

This answer is incorrect. The passage states that crops used for feeding people will be needed for the production of biofuels but this does not suggest that there will be food shortages. Overall it would be a poor conclusion to draw from this passage.

C Biofuels may not necessarily help tackle global warming.

This is the correct answer as the passage puts forward the arguments on both sides of the debate about the use of biofuels and global warming. Which indicates that the negatives may equal the positives in terms of pollution and energy use.

D Alternative crop production methods are necessary to reduce carbon emissions.

This answer is incorrect as alternative methods of crop production is not discussed in the passage. One could conclude that this potentially could be the answer to the problem of biofuel production but it would not be the best conclusion of the information available.

E The carbon use reduction targets on all countries is obligatory.

This answer is incorrect and is not supported by the information in the passage and is therefore irrelevant to the argument.

37 A round box of chocolates with a diameter of 40 cm and a depth of 3 cm is gift wrapped and tied with a 250 cm length of ribbon which is tied in a bow on top as shown below. After completion of the gift wrapping 60 cm of ribbon was left.

Bottom   Side   Top

A second piece of ribbon also measuring 250 cm is used to decorate a second gift. The ribbon is tied in a similar bow to the first gift and all the ribbon is used.

How many boxes of chocolates are there in the second gift?

A 6

B 10

C 5

D 4

E 12

Question 37: answer and rationale

Extracting relevant information and multi-stage calculations: rule
This question contains addition, multiplication and division.

The highlighted statement and rationale is correct.

> **A   6**
>
> This answer is correct.
>
> *Step 1:* the question contains information that is irrelevant to the calculation, to answer the question the only relevant measures are the depth of the box 3 cm and the amount of extra ribbon available for use 60 cm.
>
> *Step 2:* from the diagrams it can be seen that the ribbon crosses the depth of the box four times, therefore 3 cm × 4 = 12 cm, therefore each additional box will use up 12 cm more of the ribbon.
>
> *Step 3:* calculate the number of additional boxes of chocolates, 60 cm of extra ribbon divided by 12 cm required for each box = 5, add this to the original box = 6.

B   10

This answer is incorrect and would indicate a miscalculation.

C   5

This answer is incorrect and would equal the additional boxes only.

D   4

This answer is incorrect and would indicate a miscalculation.

E   12

This answer is incorrect and would indicate that the depth of the box has only been counted twice instead of four times.

38 This question relates to the passage on page 57.

Which one of the following is the best statement of the flaw in the above argument?

A   It does not take into account the profound effect the weather can have on the tide.

B   It ignores the fact that some areas only have one tide.

C   The assumption made is one of cause and effect.

D   It overlooks spring tides when the lunar and solar tides line up.

E   It ignores the fact that strong winds and abnormal atmospheric pressure makes it impossible to predict tide levels.

Question 38: answer and rationale

This question requires that you can identify the **flaw** in the argument presented in the passage. This is an evaluation as to whether the options provided best describe the flaw in the argument, in other words are they true or false in relation to the question. In order to address this question it will be necessary to read the passage thoroughly in order to reach a conclusion as to which option would constitute the main flaw in the argument. The options may all appear feasible but you must decide which one option would question the whole premise. The highlighted statement and rationale is correct.

A   It does not take into account the profound effect the weather can have on the tide.

This answer is incorrect on the basis of the information available in the passage. That is not to say that the statement itself is inaccurate.

B   It ignores the fact that some areas only have one tide.

This answer is incorrect and is irrelevant in terms of the question being asked.

C   The assumption made is one of cause and effect.

This is the correct answer as the assumption being made is that the level of the alternating tides is created by the gravitational pull of the moon on the earth which is basically cause and effect.

D   It overlooks spring tides when the lunar and solar tides line up.

This answer is incorrect as the passage does not make reference to spring tides and for this statement to be correct external knowledge would have to be applied.

E   It ignores the fact that strong winds and abnormal atmospheric pressure makes it impossible to predict tide levels.

This answer is incorrect and could not be arrived at without applying further information.

39 A game has two bags of balls. Bag 'A' contains four red balls and four blue balls. Bag 'B' contains four red bats and four blue bats.

To play a game you have to have a matching red bat and red ball which are drawn from the bags whilst blindfolded. To achieve this what is the *least* number of bats and balls you must draw from the bags?

A   Five balls and one bat.

B   Three balls and three bats.

C   Four balls and four bats.

D   Five balls and four bats.

E   Five balls and five bats.

Question 39: answer and rationale

Dependent events and random: rule

This question is based on dependent events, in other words, the probabilities of the second event will be influenced by the outcomes of the first event and so on. However, random events will also influence the outcome and this random effect has to be eliminated.

The highlighted statement and rationale is correct.

A   Five balls and one bat.

This answer is incorrect. It is certain that you would have a matching bat and ball but they could be either blue or red and therefore the outcome is not certain.

B   Three balls and three bats.

This answer is incorrect and it would depend on the luck of the draw which could result in a red bat and ball but might not and therefore the outcome is not certain.

C   Four balls and four bats.

This answer is incorrect and it would depend on the luck of the draw which could result in a red bat and ball but might not and therefore the outcome is not certain.

D   Five balls and four bats.

This answer is incorrect as the blindfolded draw of the bat could result in four blue bats being drawn.

E   Five balls and five bats.

This answer is correct.

Step 1: if the first ball drawn from Bag 'A' is blue then the probability of drawing a red ball is increased, and so on, but as the balls are being drawn at random then there is always a possibility that four blue balls will be drawn before a red one or vice versa. Therefore, five balls must be drawn to ensure the draw of a red ball.

Step 2: the draw for a bat will be dependent on the same principle as the draw for the balls and the first four bats drawn could be blue therefore you will still have to draw five bats to ensure having a red bat.

40 This question relates to the passage on page 57.

Which one of the following statements, if true, would most support the above argument?

A   Hitler's diaries captured the imagination of the world press/public.

B   Forgeries of famous people's work are eventually uncovered.

C   The work created by forgers provides a lucrative outcome.

D   Until the diaries were proved to be forgeries they were generally regarded as genuine.

E   The diaries of the infamous will always attract interest and a high price.

Question 40: answer and rationale

This question requires that you can identify which statement, **if factual**, would most support the power of the argument presented in the passage. This is an evaluation as to whether the options provided, if they were true, would most strengthen the argument. In order to address this question it will be necessary to read the passage thoroughly in order to arrive at the most logical answer. The options may all appear feasible but you must decide which one option would be the most likely. The highlighted statement and rationale is correct.

A   **Hitler's diaries captured the imagination of the world press/public.**

This is an incorrect answer as it is explicit already in the passage that this was the case.

B   **Forgeries of famous people's work are eventually uncovered.**

This is an incorrect answer and whilst it may be true that most forgeries are eventually uncovered it would only support the latter part of the passage.

C   The work created by forgers provides a lucrative outcome.

This is an incorrect answer and would not support the argument in the passage as the forgeries were identified and the gains to those who produced them may have been minimal or they could have even been caught.

> D   Until the diaries were proved to be forgeries they were generally regarded as genuine.
>
> This is the correct answer as the considerable interest in the diaries and the use of extracts from them would suggest that this statement is true.

E   The diaries of the infamous will always attract interest and a high price.

This answer is incorrect and would only support the fact that there was considerable interest in the Hitler diaries but as these were found to be forgeries this statement is not supported in the passage.

41   Below is a table detailing golf buggy hire.

TIGER GOLF CLUB
Summer buggy hire
7 am – 8 pm, 7 days per week

HOURLY RATE	
7 am – 5 pm	£3.50 per hour
5 pm – 8 pm	£2.25 per hour
½ day hire 7 am – 1 pm	£16.00
All day hire	£20.00
Refundable deposit £20.00	

How much will it cost to hire a golf buggy from 2 pm for 5 hours?

A   £17.50

B   £16.00

C   £15.00

D   £20.00

E   £11.25

Question 41: answer and rationale

Extracting information and multi-stage calculations: rule
This question requires that you can extract the relevant information and perform multiplication and addition.

The highlighted statement and rationale is correct.

A   £17.50

This answer is incorrect as it would be the result of 5 hours at £3.50 and 2 hours of the required hire time are at the lesser rate of £2.25.

B   £16.00

This answer is incorrect as it is the ½ day hire rate of £16 between 7 am and 1 pm which is too early for the required hire time.

C   £15.00

This answer is correct.

Step 1: extract the relevant information, buggy hire from 2 pm for 5 hours, 2 pm to 5 pm = 3 hours × £3.50 = £10.50, 5 pm to 7 pm = 2 hours × £2.25 = £4.50.

Step 2: add hire rates, £10.50 + £4.50 = £15 (note the refundable deposit is redundant information as it is not an actual cost.)

D   £20.00

This answer is incorrect as it is the rate for a full day hire which would exceed the rate for 5 hours.

E   £11.25

This answer is incorrect as it is the rate for 5 hours commencing at 5 pm which is too late for the required hire.

42   This question relates to the passage on page 58.

Which one of the statements below is an underlying assumption of the above passage?

A   People who are concerned about animal cruelty do not eat battery-reared chickens.

B   The majority of chefs only use free-range chickens.

C   Free-range chickens are less cruelly treated than battery-reared chickens.

D   All chickens should be treated humanely.

E   Fewer people are buying battery-reared chickens.

Question 42: answer and rationale

An **assumption** is a proposition that is taken for granted, that is, as if it were known to be true. It is a statement that can be surmised or postulated given the overall context of the passage. This question is asking you to identify which statement can be surmised or postulated from the passage. In identifying an **assumption** the correct statement will not actually be stated in the passage so it is for you to determine the main argument and look for the reasoning to support this conclusion. You need to read the passage carefully to identify the overall argument and determine which one option best answers the question posed. The highlighted statement and rationale is correct.

A People who are concerned about animal cruelty do not eat battery-reared chickens.

This is an incorrect answer and cannot be assumed from the content of the passage otherwise there would be no need to campaign for the case for free-range chickens.

B The majority of chefs only use free-range chickens.

This is an incorrect answer and cannot be assumed that just because the passage mentions that a celebrity chef is fronting the campaign this can be generalised to the majority.

C Free-range chickens are less cruelly treated than battery-reared chickens.

This is the correct answer as it is clearly an underlying assumption of the passage that free-range chickens are less cruelly treated, due to the campaign to encourage consumers to buy only them.

D All chickens should be treated humanely.

This is an incorrect answer and would constitute a value judgement not an assumption.

E Fewer people are buying battery-reared chickens.

This is an incorrect answer and is obviously not an underlying assumption of the passage hence there would be no need to campaign.

43 June is helping her dad pack bait for his pest control business. The bait is in 10 g packets. June asks her dad how many packets of bait he needs. Her dad informs her that he sets 20 traps and places 20 g of bait in each trap. He works an 8 hour day and he checks all the traps every hour. During the first 5 hours he has to add 10 g of bait to half the traps each hour. During the last 3 hours he has to add 5 g of bait to three-quarters of the traps. If there is a part packet left he adds it to the last trap.

How many packets of bait does June need to pack for her dad?

A 58

B 37.5

C 38

D 57.5

E 60

Question 43: answer and rationale

Multi-stage calculation: rule

This question requires that you can perform multiplication, division, and addition.

The highlighted statement and rationale is correct.

> A 58
>
> This answer is correct.
>
> *Step 1:* 1 packet = 10 g, 20 traps × 20 g (2 packets) = 40 packets.
>
> *Step 2:* 10 g (1 packet) is added to half the traps during the first 5 hours, 20 ÷ 2 = 10 traps × 10 g (1 packet) = 10 packets.
>
> *Step 3:* 5 g (½ packet) is added to three quarters of the traps during the last 3 hours, 20 ÷ 4 × 3 = 15 traps × 5 g (½ packet) = 7½ packets.
>
> *Step 4:* remaining ½ packet is added to last trap, therefore total = 40 + 10 + 7½ + ½ = 58

B 37.5

This answer is incorrect and is would not be sufficient to set the 20 g in each of the 20 traps at the start of the day and can be dismissed immediately.

C 38

This answer is incorrect and is would not be sufficient to set the 20 g in each of the 20 traps at the start of the day and can be dismissed immediately.

D   57.5

This answer is incorrect as the remaining part packet (½), has not been added.

E   60

This answer is incorrect as you are not being asked to round up to the nearest ten.

44 This question relates to the passage on page 59.

Which one of the following statements, if true, would detract from the above argument?

A   The number of people contracting STDs will decrease in the future.

B   Providing educational resources for health management is expensive.

C   National Health Service Trusts have increased expenditure on STD educational programmes at the same level as AIDS programmes.

D   The social stigma attached to people who contract STDs will diminish over time.

E   Further scientific advances will reduce the medical interventions required for people with STDs.

Question 44: answer and rationale

This question requires that you can identify which statement, **if factual**, would detract from the power of the argument presented in the passage. This is an evaluation as to whether the options provided, if they were true, would most weaken the argument. In order to address this question it will be necessary to read the passage thoroughly in order to arrive at the most logical answer. The options may all appear feasible but you must decide which one option would be the most likely. The highlighted statement and rationale is correct.

A   The number of people contracting STDs will decrease in the future.

This is the correct answer given the content of the passage and the statistical fact that the spread of STDs has increased year on year since accurate records were first kept it would be true that a decrease in the numbers would contradict the argument.

B   Providing educational resources for health management is expensive.

This answer is incorrect as the costs of health management are probably the main reason for the lack of educational programmes designed to reduce or eliminate STDs and if this statement were true then it would support the argument and not detract from it.

C   National Health Service Trusts have increased expenditure on STD educational programmes at the same level as AIDS programmes.

This answer is incorrect as the passage indicates that the expenditure on STD educational programmes is less and even if it were true then it would support rather than detract from the argument.

D   The social stigma attached to people who contract STDs will diminish over time.

This answer is incorrect as the claim that the social stigma attached to STDs has lessened and that it will diminish further over time forms part of the argument as to why there is a lack of adequate educational resources to reduce or eliminate them.

E   Further scientific advances will reduce the medical interventions required for people with STDs.

This answer is incorrect because if this were true then this would give substance to the view that the obligations to educational programmes are not as great as they were.

45   A cube has sides that each measure 40 cm in length.

What is the volume of the cube?

A   0.064 m

B   0.064 m^2

C   0.16 m^2

D   64,000 cm^3

E   1,600 cm^2

Question 45: answer and rationale

Volume: rule
To find the volume of a cuboid multiply the length by the width by the height.

The highlighted statement and rationale is correct.

A   0.064 m

This answer is incorrect has it has the incorrect units of m instead of cm^3.

B   0.064 m^2

This answer is incorrect has it has the incorrect units m^2 instead of cm^3.

C   0.16 m²

This answer is incorrect has it has the incorrect units m² instead of cm³.

D   64,000 cm³

This is the correct answer.

Step 1: the length of each side is 40 cm therefore the volume is 40 × 40 × 40 = 64,000 cm³. This answer is also the only options that has the correct units, namely cm³.

E   1,600 cm²

This answer is incorrect as it is the area of one side of the cube and therefore it has the incorrect units of cm² instead of cm³.

46 This question relates to the passage on page 60.

Which one of the following statements most closely mirrors the reasoning of the above argument?

A   If the present level of storm and flood damage does not end soon then insurance companies will be inundated with claims. Some insurance companies may struggle to meet the level of claims and payments could take some time. If storm and flood damage become a feature of our climate insurance companies may add extra clauses to policies.

B   If the cost of fuel continues to rise, then people will be more economical and will buy less fuel. The fuel prices will then stop increasing if less fuel is purchased. Therefore, the rise in fuel prices must peak soon.

C   If we do not pay our skilled workers more many of them will seek work abroad. We will then be left with a national skills shortage. Therefore, wages for skilled workers must increase if we wish to maintain a high skills base in this country.

D   If we are all prepared to pay more road tax, then the government could afford to improve the road network. An improved road network would result in shorter more cost effective transport. Therefore, if we want a more efficient road system, we must be prepared to pay higher road tax.

E   The UK car industry has been downsizing for some time. If the industry continues to decrease job losses will be high. Towns and cities whose economies depend on the salaries of car workers would suffer as a consequence. If the decline in the car industry continues then these towns and cities will badly affected.

Question 46: answer and rationale

This question requires that you can examine the passage and identify a similarity in the structure or pattern of the argument that is reproduced in the correct statement. The highlighted statement and rationale is correct.

A   If the present level of storm and flood damage does not end soon then insurance companies will be inundated with claims. Some insurance companies may struggle to meet the level of claims and payments could take some time. If storm and flood damage become a feature of our climate insurance companies may add extra clauses to policies.

This answer is incorrect as the economic impact highlighted in this statement is due to what could be termed 'acts of god' or naturally occurring problems which are outside the realms of control.

B   If the cost of fuel continues to rise, then people will be more economical and will buy less fuel. The fuel prices will then stop increasing if less fuel is purchased. Therefore, the rise in fuel prices must peak soon.

This answer is incorrect as it is more a statement about the economies of supply and demand.

C   If we do not pay our skilled workers more many of them will seek work abroad. We will then be left with a national skills shortage. Therefore, wages for skilled workers must increase if we wish to maintain a high skills base in this country.

This answer is incorrect as again it is related to a supply and demand situation.

D   If we are all prepared to pay more road tax, then the government could afford to improve the road network. An improved road network would result in shorter more cost effective transport. Therefore, if we want a more efficient road system, we must be prepared to pay higher road tax.

This answer is incorrect as it relates to paying more for an improved service which is a completely different economic argument to the one in the passage.

E   The UK car industry has been downsizing for some time. If the industry continues to decrease job losses will be high. Towns and cities whose economies depend on the salaries of car workers would suffer as a consequence. If the decline in the car industry continues then these towns and cities will badly affected.

This is the correct answer as it is most closely mirrors the economic argument in the passage caused by recession.

47 Jane buys biscuits once a fortnight for her grandmother. Her grandmother's favourite biscuits are 96p per packet and she gives Jane enough money for her usual fortnightly supply. At the supermarket there is a multi-buy offer on 10 packets or more. This reduces the packets by 16p each and Jane realises that her grandmother can now have two more packets of biscuits.

How many packets of biscuits does she buy?

A   10

B   12

C   14

D   16

E   20

Question 47: answer and rationale

Multi-stage calculation: rule
This question contains subtraction, multiplication and addition.

The highlighted statement and rationale is correct.

A   10

This answer is incorrect as it would equate to the number of packets of biscuits Jane could buy before the multi-buy offer.

B   12

This answer is correct.

Step 1: calculate the multi-buy offer price, 96p per packet – 16p reduction = offer price of 80p per packet.

Step 2: Jane realises she can buy her grandmother two more packets at the reduced rate, 2 × 80p = £1.60 which is equal 16p × 10, therefore Jane must have originally had enough money to buy 10 packets.

Step 3: 10 packets + 2 packets = 12 packets

C   14

This answer is incorrect and would indicate a miscalculation.

D   16

This answer is incorrect as the value 16 only relates to the 16p reduction in price.

E   20

This answer is incorrect and would indicate a gross miscalculation.

48 This question relates to the passage on page 61.

Which one of the following statements best expresses the main premise of the above argument?

A   The mortality rate for children should further decrease in the future.

B   Eating fresh fruit and vegetables significantly reduces the likelihood of disease.

C   Medical science has been responsible for increasing life expectancy.

D   There will be a decrease in the rate of illnesses associated with adulthood.

E   Availability of food products has been the most important contributor to child mortality levels.

Question 48: answer and rationale

This question requires that you can identify the **main premise** of the argument in the passage. It does not suggest that other ideas will not be present. Again this is an evaluation as to whether the options provided are the main idea, in other words are they true or false in relation to the question. In order to address this question it will be necessary to read the passage thoroughly in order to follow the ideas and the structure of the argument to reach a conclusion as to which option is the fundamental idea. The passage may contain several points that are pertinent to the overall argument as they help to build up the body of evidence. Therefore, it is important to examine the structure of the argument as this may indicate where the **main** premise is positioned. The highlighted statement and rationale is correct.

A   **The mortality rate for children should further decrease in the future.**

This is the correct answer as the main premise of the argument in the passage relates to how advances in science and diet have improved mortality rates for children which should improve further as the technology is spread to other areas of the world.

B   Eating fresh fruit and vegetables significantly reduces the likelihood of disease.

This is an incorrect answer as it only forms part of the argument put forward for the increase in health and well-being.

C   Medical science has been responsible for increasing life expectancy.

This again is an incorrect answer as it only forms part of the argument put forward for the increase in health and well-being.

D   There will be a decrease in the rate of illnesses associated with adulthood.

This answer is incorrect even though the arguments put forward do suggest that this has been another outcome as a result of the advances made.

E   Availability of food products has been the most important contributor to child mortality levels.

This again is an incorrect answer as it only forms part of the argument put forward for the reduction in mortality levels.

49 I am having friends round this evening for a barbeque. Some of my friends are vegetarian and I can't cook their veggie burgers and veggie sausage with the meat ones. We are due to eat at 7.00 pm and I have drawn up a timed 'To Do' list as follows:

'TO DO' LIST

Make beef burgers and skewer sausages 15 minutes

Barbeque beef burgers and sausages 30 minutes

Cut bread rolls 10 minutes

Make salad dressing 10 minutes

Wash salad 5 minutes

Toss salad in dressing 5 minutes

Make veggie burgers and veggie sausages 30 minutes

Barbeque veggie burgers and veggie sausages 30 minutes

Put veggie food in hot store 5 minutes

Put out patio furniture and lay the table 15 minutes

My barbeque has one grill area and an area for storing hot food. I will serve the food as soon as the meat burgers and sausages are cooked.

What is the latest time I should start preparing the food?

A   5.10 pm

B   5.25 pm

C   5.30 pm

D   4.25 pm

E   5.20 pm

Question 49: answer and rationale

Extracting relevant information and basic calculation: rule
This question requires that you can extract relevant information and avoid any distracting information. Basic addition and subtraction are then required.

A   5.10 pm

This answer is incorrect as it would possibly indicate that tasks that could be carried out during cooking time have been included.

B   5.25 pm

This answer is correct.

Step 1: extract the relevant information, some friends are vegetarian, due to eat at 7.00 pm, one grill and an area for storing, serve as soon as meat burgers and sausages are cooked, what is the latest time to start preparing.

Step 2: vegetarian burgers and sausages have to be made and cooked first to avoid contamination, 30 minutes preparation + 30 minutes cooking time + 5 minutes to store when cooked = 1 hour 5 minutes.

Step 3: making the beef burgers and skewering the sausages 15 minutes + washing the salad 5 minutes and + making the salad dressing 10 minute = 30 minutes, which can be carried out whilst the vegetarian option is cooking and therefore does not need to be added to the total time.

Step 4: the beef burgers and sausages take 30 minutes to barbeque and during this time the bread can be cut (10 minutes) and the patio furniture, etc. put out (15 minutes), which leaves 5 minutes spare until the meat is cooked.

Step 5: calculate total time required, 1 hour 5 minutes + 30 minutes = 1 hour 35 minutes, therefore the latest time to begin preparing the food is 7.00 pm − 1 hour 35 minutes = 5.25 pm.

C   5.30 pm

This answer is incorrect and would possibly indicate that the time required to store the vegetarian food has not been added to the total.

D   4.25 pm

This answer is incorrect and would possibly indicate that all the times from the 'To Do List' have been added into the total.

E   5.20 pm

This answer is incorrect and would indicate a possible miscalculation.

50 This question relates to the passage on page 62.

Which one of the following statements is an underlying assumption of the above argument?

A   All religions believe in reincarnation.

B   Mediums can make contact with people who are dead.

C   Those who believe in the spirit world are often relatives of the recently bereaved.

D   Mediums, fortune-tellers and astrologers have extra-sensory perception.

E   Talking to dead loved ones is a comfort to surviving relations and friends.

Question 50: answer and rationale

An **assumption** is a proposition that is taken for granted, that is, as if it were known to be true. It is a statement that can be surmised or postulated given the overall context of the passage. This question is asking you to identify which statement can be surmised or postulated from the passage. In identifying an **assumption** the correct statement will not actually be stated in the passage so it is for you to determine the main argument and look for the reasoning to support this conclusion. You need to read the passage carefully to identify the overall argument and determine which one option best answers the question posed. The highlighted statement and rationale is correct.

A   All religions believe in reincarnation.

This is an incorrect answer as the passage refers to life after death in terms of the 'spirit world' and not reincarnation in some other life form therefore this assumption could not be made.

B   Mediums can make contact with people who are dead.

This is an incorrect answer. The passage indicates that there are mediums who purport to communicate with those who are dead but one could not assume that this statement is true from the content of the passage.

C   Those who believe in the spirit world are often relatives of the recently bereaved.

This is an incorrect answer as the assumption cannot be made that the relations and friends referred to in the passage actually believe in the spirit world even though they make use of mediums.

D   Mediums, fortune-tellers and astrologers have extra-sensory perception.

This is an incorrect answer as the statements made in the passage about mediums, fortune-tellers and astrologers make no claims to the truth let alone alluding to the powers of extra-sensory perception.

E   Talking to dead loved ones is a comfort to surviving relations and friends.

This is the correct answer as the assumption can be made from the passage that those relations or friends who seek out mediums, etc. do take comfort from communications with the dead whatever the case may or may not be in reality for the efficacy of such liaisons. If this were not true then there would be no call for their services.

Chapter 5
TSA Writing Task

17. Introduction

The Writing Task is only used by the University of Oxford TSA and not by Cambridge.

It is as important to prepare for this part of the TSA as it is for the Thinking Skills Assessment. Firstly, the type of questions with which you will be confronted may be very different from what you have been used to in your previous educational experiences. Second, the time constraint of 30 minutes really does focus the mind and you need to develop the skills of structure and content within this constraint.

This section is extremely relevant to your application as the Writing Task has been included by Oxford specifically to test the skills that they consider will be important for your degree programme. Your product from this task should demonstrate that you have the ability or potential ability to:

- recognise and resolve conflict
- formulate and provide valid support for logical arguments
- consider alternative explanations for difficult ideas.

Probably the most singular thing you can do to prepare for this task is to read a variety of broadsheet newspapers and keep up to date through magazines, periodicals, etc., both generally and specifically in relation to your preferred subject(s) (i.e. intended degree subjects). These 'quality' newspapers, magazines, etc. often provide conflicting views and arguments on a range of topical issues that will undoubtedly be the subject of one or more of the writing task questions. The more familiar you are with these views and arguments the better you should perform. Obviously, it would be preferable to get into a routine of reading broadsheet newspapers over a period of several months rather than a week or two before the assessment!

18. TSA Writing Task

The TSA Writing Task requires you to write a single short essay within 30 minutes. Normally three essay questions are provided from which you select only one. The essay questions will be on general subjects that do not require any specialised knowledge.

At the outset of the task you will be provided with a set of instructions and a separate answer booklet for your essay. Two blank pages are provided within the answer booklet that you can use for making notes before writing the essay. More information about this task can be found on the Oxford website.

Each of the three essay questions are followed by two or three statements relating directly to the question and which should be addressed in the essay.

Here are two examples of the type of question and additional statements with which you might be presented:

1. What are the arguments for and against the introduction of proportional representation in general elections?

    Write a unified essay to address this question, in which you consider the following:

    Who would gain and who would lose by proportional representation?

    Would minor parties have an inequitable say in the government of the country?

    Why are governments elected by proportional representation seen as ineffective?

2. The international agreements on the emission of greenhouse gases are ineffective. How would you respond to this statement?

    Write a unified essay to address this question, in which you consider the following:

    What are the competing issues of the world's superpowers in relation to controlling greenhouse gas emissions?

    Who will be the losers if the international agreements are effective?

    Who should be leading the way on climate change action?

19. Structured approach

It is important that each of the following stages is considered separately before you attempt writing the essay:

- Identify what is being asked in each of the questions
- Identify the question that you would be best able to answer
- Brainstorm the issues and arguments relevant to the question
- Plan the structure
- Write the essay
- Revision

You may be one of those people in the top few percent of the population who can just write a well-reasoned essay without any preparation or planning. If you are not then time spent on the first four stages will be time well spent before you start actually writing the essay. Give yourself up to 5 MINUTES for these four stages, probably a couple of minutes for the first two stages and 3 minutes for the next stages. Control your natural urge to skip these stages to ensure you properly plan and prepare – as the old saying goes, 'failing to plan is planning to fail!'

Identifying the question

At the outset you may convince yourself that you know next to nothing about any of the essay questions on offer. DON'T PANIC! No matter what the subject there will be very few occasions where you are unable to come up with a number of relevant ideas to form a useful structure from your own knowledge and experience and invariably this is the process that is of interest to the examiners.

In your anxiety you will want to get on with writing the essay but you should resist this temptation and spend a few minutes making sure you will be answering the question being asked. The question will usually provide you with both the structure of the essay and sometimes the abilities you are required to display.

It sounds obvious, but it is important to be absolutely sure what the question is asking you to do. It has often been the case that a person reads into the question something that isn't there and so writes the whole essay without answering the question.

Let's look at the example essay topics given above and unpack them to determine what is being asked:

1. **What are the arguments for and against the introduction of proportional representation in general elections?'**

    This question can be broken down easily into four constituent parts, i.e. *'What are the arguments/for and against/the introduction of proportional representation/in general elections?'*

    'What are the arguments' is essentially asking for the reasons *for and against the introduction of proportional representation.* Reasons include evidence, principles, assumptions and logical inferences or causal connections which are given to support judgements and recommendations. Further details about arguments, reasons and conclusions are provided under the heading 'developing writing techniques'.

    'for and against' is asking for the pros and cons of *the introduction of proportional representation . . .* This is not asking you for your own ideas and thoughts on the issue and you need to keep focused on what is being asked.

'*the introduction of proportional representation/in general elections*' are both very specific and your arguments must retain a focus on these.

2. **What is your response to the view that the international agreements on the emission of greenhouse gases are ineffective?**

    This question can be broken down into five constituent parts, though the last two parts might preferably be combined, i.e.

    '*What is your response/to the view/that the international agreements/on the emission of greenhouse gases/are ineffective?*'

    '*What is your response*' is asking for your reaction to the question posed. It invites you to present both evidence, principles, assumptions and logical inferences, as well as your own thoughts on the issue.

    '*to the view*' is suggesting that there are apparently opposing views to the one given and they should be raised and considered in the essay.

    '*that the international agreements*' is quite specific and in answering this question you would need to demonstrate a certain amount of knowledge in this area.

    '*on the emission of greenhouse gases*' is quite specific and in answering the question you would need to demonstrate a certain amount of knowledge of the causes and impact of the emission of greenhouse gases.

    '*are ineffective*' is making a definitive statement which should be considered in that light and contested or otherwise.

The two examples given above may appear somewhat long-winded. In reality this would not be the case. It would probably take less than a minute to identify and note down the constituent parts of any particular question to make sure your essay will directly answer the chosen question.

There may be more than one question that you feel able to answer but you need to consider which one would allow you best to demonstrate your analytical abilities. The examiners are looking for a 'well-reasoned' essay.

Some questions may lend themselves to a more 'argumentative' approach, examining the various pros and cons of the issue(s) raised and forming some kind of conclusions, for example, in relation to the 'sample essays' above, the question, '*What are the arguments for and against the introduction of proportional representation in general elections?*'

Other questions may require a more analytical or critical approach requiring you to show you can identify more difficult abstract concepts, for example, in relation to the 'sample essays' above the question, '*What is your response to the view that the international agreements on the emission of greenhouse gases are ineffective?*' Both types of questions will obviously influence the way in which your essay is structured and some type of structure should already be forming in your mind, even subconsciously, before you move onto the next stage.

Brainstorming the issues

There is no doubt that when universities examine essays they are looking for good analytical ability in order to distinguish between better performers. It is suggested by some academic writers that analysis and brainstorming are two separate concepts. In analysis the individual identifies and analyses the concepts and implications of the question. They then write down their own ideas identifying the concepts' essential characteristics. In the other concept the individual is simply brainstorming their own ideas. The analysis concept requires considerable time to unravel and consequently is not advised for use in essays under test conditions.

Brainstorming is coming up with a number of ideas from your own knowledge and experience and writing them down even if they are not relevant. You can easily discard the irrelevant ideas afterwards. Essentially, the product of brainstorming will provide the basis for the essay structure and the content.

There are a number of different techniques available when brainstorming: it can be totally organic and unstructured, or more structured methods such as mind-mapping and the use of mnemonics can be used. You may be familiar with or used to a particular method and if so use it. Some people find mind-mapping beneficial, others don't. If you haven't previously used this method and it appeals to you buy a book on it; there are plenty available. We will concentrate on the assistance to brainstorming that can be provided by mnemonics in relation to essay writing.

Children are often taught to remember the colours of the rainbow using the mnemonic, 'Richard of York gave battle in vain' – red, orange, yellow, green, blue, indigo and violet. Students would normally use mnemonics where they are learnt for specific knowledge-based examinations.

However, there are two useful mnemonics that are often used for providing a structure into which you can place your ideas and thoughts or which themselves supply a vehicle and structure for encouraging such ideas and thoughts.

The first mnemonic, often useful in answering 'argue for and against' type questions, though also used for more open questions, is referred to as a **SWOT** analysis – **S**trengths, **W**eaknesses, **O**pportunities and **T**hreats.

We will use this mnemonic in examining the example essay question, '*What are the arguments for and against the introduction of proportional representation in general elections?*'

Strengths:	May encourage people to vote
	More representative government
Weaknesses:	Hung parliaments
	Lack of leadership
	Weak government
Opportunities:	Focus on the needs of the electorate
	Policies represent the needs of the electorate
	Greater democracy
	More say in government
	Liberal Democrats manifesto
Threats:	Policies become ineffective
	Government over-representative of minority groups
	All talk and no action

The second mnemonic provides a broad 'analysis' of a question and is referred to as **PESTEL** analysis – **P**olitical, **E**conomic, **S**ocial, **T**echnical, **E**nvironmental and **L**egal.

We will use this mnemonic in examining the example essay question, '*What is your response to the view that the international agreements on the emission of greenhouse gases are ineffective?*'

Political:	Kyoto Agreement (international)
	USA not signatory
	Welfare
	Electability
Economic:	Cost benefit
	Developing countries
	Employment
	Demography
Social:	Health
	Employment
	Leisure
	Transport
Technical:	Other energy sources
Environmental:	Ozone depletion in stratosphere
	Greenhouse gases in the troposphere
	Transport
Legal:	Treaties
	Compensation
	Enforcement/sanctions

Ideas are organic in that they grow and develop over time. Consequently, at stages throughout your writing other ideas will come to you that have not been included in the structure. You may consider that some of these ideas are sufficiently important to issues or arguments you have raised that it is essential they are included. When you think of them note them on one of the blank pages provided so that you don't forget them. These additional ideas can often be inserted within the final section of the essay where you are providing a summary or synthesis of the issues or arguments.

Planning the structure

Whatever technique you have used to brainstorm your chosen question you should now have sufficient material with which to plan your structure.

The Writing Task questions provided by Oxford in fact provide the outline structure for your essay. In relation to the example question '*The international agreements on the emission of greenhouse gases are ineffective. How would you respond to this statement?*' you are required to consider the following three questions:

- What are the competing issues of the world's superpowers in relation to controlling greenhouse gas emissions?
- Who will be the losers if the international agreements are effective?
- Who should be leading the way on climate change action?

It therefore follows that your essay should be structured in three specific parts in order to answer these three questions.

Although it seems pretty obvious, all essays need a beginning, middle and an end, but it is surprising how often even good students forget this rule. A useful way to apply this rule is as follows:

The beginning is: **tell them what you're going to tell them.**

The opening paragraph or paragraphs gives the reader, in this case an examiner, advance notice of the overall direction and substance of your essay.

The middle is: **tell them.**

Tell them the answer to the question which, if using the mnemonic structure, would include the substance of the SWOT or PESTEL analysis.

The end is: **tell them what you've told them.**

In this part you can summarise or synthesise your arguments or analysis, that is, '*What is your response to the view that the international agreements on the emission of greenhouse gases are ineffective?*'

20. Writing the essay

The most effective way of creating a structure is by the use of paragraphs. There will be a paragraph for the introduction, separate paragraphs for each of the 'arguments' and a paragraph for the conclusion. You are not writing a short story with its discursive narrative; you are providing an analysis of the question and developing reasoned arguments.

The content of the introductory paragraph is very important. It provides the opportunity to grab the attention of the reader. The introduction will reflect how good or bad the rest of the essay is going to be and how it will be perceived by an examiner who has many more ahead of him or her! It must set the scene and give a direction as to what can be expected in the body of the essay (not in the conclusion).

In relation to paragraphing the 'arguments', where you are considering 'arguments' and 'counter-arguments', you may prefer to present these opposing views in separate paragraphs.

There is no hard and fast rule about the length of paragraphs though it is suggested that varying their length does make the essay more readable. Whatever, don't get hung up about it and concentrate on the content of the essay not the length of paragraphs.

The structure of a paragraph is not a science but a simple rule of consistency that will make sure you stick to the game plan and not waffle on about irrelevant matters. This rule of consistency is in three parts. Normally the opening part of a paragraph will be where you describe the issue or argument that the paragraph will cover. The second part is where you develop on this issue or argument, providing a better understanding of what you're talking about. The third part is providing the evidence in relation to the issue or argument.

Writing the concluding paragraph should be the easiest part of your essay. What you have stated in your essay can be pulled together in the conclusion, for example, do the pros outweigh the cons? However, it is seen as beneficial if the conclusion is as thought-provoking as possible. This might include discussing the wider implications of the issue, what might happen if the issue remains unresolved, or what you consider could be done to resolve the issue.

One other simple rule is KEEP IT SIMPLE! Think of books you have read where the author appears to be with you and talking to you. Writing is like talking but in print. When you have thought about what you want to say in your essay, say it as clearly as you can. Keep your sentences as short as possible and read them back to yourself when you've written them to make sure they say what you intended.

Throughout your writing remember that time is of the essence: you only have 30 minutes to write the essay, so keep it concise and accurate.

A final word – there is no doubt that examiners should be more concerned with the content of the essay and not the format, grammar, punctuation and spelling. This may be true but an essay that is pleasing on the eye and easier to read and understand must affect the examiner's approach, even subconsciously. After all they are only human!

21. Critical thinking

This section provides a brief overview of critical thinking, the components of which are useful *per se* but particularly to the TSA Writing Task requirement.

Critical thinking is about how we approach problems, questions and issues, and academicians have suggested it as the best way in which to get at the truth. As already stated earlier in this book, the capacity for critical thought is acknowledged as a valuable intellectual asset in higher education.

Critical thinking is not really a new concept to philosophers and scholars and has actually been around for some time in other guises. For example, in his book *The Improvement of the Mind*, published by Gale and Curtis in 1810, Isaac Watts said:

> Though observation and instruction, reading and conversation, may furnish us with many ideas of men and things, yet it is our own meditation and the labour of our own thought that must form our judgement of things. Our own thoughts should join or disjoin these ideas in a proposition for ourselves: it is our mind that must judge for ourselves concerning the agreement or disagreement of ideas, and form propositions of truth out of them. Reading and conversation may acquaint us with many truths and with many arguments to support them, but it is our own study and reasoning that must determine whether these propositions are true, and whether these arguments are just and solid.

What is critical thinking? Probably the most comprehensive and recent longitudinal study of what constitutes critical thinking was carried out in the USA and Canada. This was a two-year research project involving mainly people in the humanities, sciences, social sciences and educational field. It was conducted on behalf of the American Philosophical Association and the results were published under the title *Critical Thinking: A Statement of Expert Consensus for Purposes of Educational Assessment and Instruction*, The California Academic Press, Millbrae, CA, 1990.

The research identified a number of core critical thinking skills that include interpretation, analysis, evaluation, inference, explanation and self regulation, and these are discussed below.

Interpretation
This is about comprehension and expression. It is the ability to be able to understand and give meaning to a wide variety of things, such as a problem, situation, event, rules, procedures, etc.

Analysis

To analyse something we break something down into its constituent parts to see what it actually means. It might be examining ideas or looking for arguments such as identifying what is similar or different between approaches to the solution of a problem. It could also be about identifying unstated assumptions in an article or book.

Evaluation

When we evaluate something we are seeking to establish whether something is credible. This could be judging an author's credibility, comparing the pros and cons of alternative interpretations, or judging whether evidence supports a conclusion.

Inference

This is concerned with the skills of deduction and conclusion. It is the ability to consider information in whatever format and draw from it reasonable conclusions. This might include identifying the implications of advocating a particular position on a subject, or even developing a set of options for addressing a particular problem.

Explanation

Explanation is really self-explanatory! It is the ability to be able to explain the results of one's reasoning. For example, providing the evidence that might have led you to accept or reject a particular position on an issue.

Self-regulation

This is about consciously monitoring what you are doing. For the purposes of the essay it is to be aware of what you are actual writing. You must remain questioning of your biases and personal opinions and assumptions. Really a checking mechanism to reconsider your interpretation or judgement to be sure it is focused on what is required.

The above are considered to be the six cognitive components of critical thinking. A way of encompassing how these skills are used can probably best be demonstrated by considering the effectiveness of solicitors and barristers in our courts. They use reasons to try and convince a judge or jury of a person's guilt or innocence. They evaluate the significance of the evidence presented by the other party and analyse their arguments. They interpret evidence for their client's benefit, make inferences which may or may not be substantiated and give explanation to events or issues. It can be assumed that they are also self-regulating in relation to the protocol required by the court and their own personal biases and beliefs.

Critical thinking is not confined to the cloisters of education but can be characterised by how a person approaches life and living in general. It is something that can be learned and research has shown that there is a significant correlation between critical thinking and reading comprehension. Improvements in critical thinking are paralleled by improvements in reading comprehension.

Chapter 6
Other Oxbridge admissions tests

This section provides information about the other admissions tests required for certain degree programmes by Oxford and Cambridge. With the exception of the Biomedical Admissions Test and the National Admissions Test for Law, and of course the Thinking Skills Assessment, all the other admissions tests *only* apply to Oxford. The information provided below is purely a summary and you are advised to reference the appropriate university website and/or the relevant College for details and requirements.

22. United Kingdom Clinical Aptitude Test (UKCAT)

The United Kingdom Clinical Aptitude Test (UKCAT) is designed to help universities to make more informed choices amongst the many highly qualified applicants who apply for medical and dental degree programmes. The test has been designed to assess those skills, traits and behaviours that identify individuals who will be successful in clinical careers.

The UKCAT is an onscreen examination and comprises of five subtests:

- **Verbal Reasoning** – assesses your ability to think logically about written information and arrive at a reasoned conclusion. This obviously has similarities with the critical thinking skills element of the Thinking Skills Assessment.
- **Quantitative Reasoning** – assesses your ability to solve numerical problems and as such is very similar to the problem-solving element of the Thinking Skills Assessment.
- **Abstract Reasoning** – assesses your ability to infer relationships from information by convergent and divergent thinking.
- **Decision Analysis** – assesses your ability to decipher and make sense of coded information.
- **Non-cognitive Analysis** – assesses attributes and characteristics of robustness, empathy and integrity.

Each of these subtests are in a multiple-choice format and timed separately, the exception being the Non-cognitive subtest which has no right or wrong answers. The overall examination is delivered in less than two hours.

Note: '*Passing the UK Clinical Aptitude Test and BMAT*' is a book produced by Learning Matters to help you prepare for these admission tests.

23. Biomedical Admissions Test (BMAT)

As with the UKCAT, the BMAT is used for applicants applying for medical and dental degree programmes.

The BMAT has three sections:

- **Aptitude and Skills** – contains three separate parts: problem solving, understanding argument (critical thinking) and data analysis and influence. This is a multiple-choice question examination of about 22 questions and a total of 1 hour is allowed.
- **Scientific Knowledge and Application** – assesses factual scientific and mathematical knowledge at GCSE level. The areas tested include: human biology, cells and cellular structure, basic maths, basic physics equations, and balancing chemical equations. This is a multiple-choice question examination of about 17 questions and a total of 30 minutes is allowed.
- **Writing Task** – assesses your ability to write a short essay selecting one topic from the three provided and 30 minutes is allowed.

24. National Admissions Test for Law (LNAT)

The LNAT is a uniform test to be taken by all candidates applying for places on law degrees. Again this admissions test is intended to improve the selection process and to make it fairer to all candidates, irrespective of their educational background. However, the LNAT is also regarded, in part, as a guide, not only to the course provider, but also to the students themselves. Lawyers – particularly those involved in litigation – spend a significant amount of their time evaluating written assertions and making deductions and conclusions from them. The LNAT is intended to replicate some of the key intellectual competencies required by those wishing to practise law. If students find they are neither stimulated nor attracted by the type of reasoning presented by the LNAT, it may well be that they will not be suited to legal practice.

The LNAT consists of two parts:

- **Section A** – a critical thinking test, once again not dissimilar to the thinking skills element of the Thinking Skills Assessment. The test contains 30 multiple-choice questions to be completed within 80 minutes.
- **Section B** – to write a 'well-reasoned' essay on a subject chosen from a list of usually five titles. The time allowed for this part of the test is 40 minutes and the length of the essay should be 400–750 words.

Note: '*Passing the National Admissions Test for Law*' is a book produced by Learning Matters to help you prepare for these admission tests.

25. Other Oxford admission tests

English Literature Admissions Test (ELAT)

The ELAT is taken by all candidates applying to read English at Oxford. The admissions test will assess how far students have developed their understanding of the key skills of close reading and demonstrating this using unfamiliar material. An explanation of 'close reading' is provided on the Oxford © website, viz:

> Close reading has been defined by Elaine Showalter (in *Teaching Literature*, Blackwell: 2003) as 'slow reading, a deliberate attempt to . . . pay attention to language, imagery, allusion, intertextuality, syntax and form' (p. 98). Earlier in the same book she writes: 'The close reading process, or *explication de texte*, that we use in analyzing literary texts does not have to come with the ponderous baggage of the New Criticism, or with political labels. Before or along with attention to factors outside the text, students have to understand something about the verbal, formal, and structural elements of the words themselves (p. 56).

As the test uses material in the form of poetry and passages that will be unfamiliar to candidates no background reading is required though the techniques of comparative analysis that form the basis of the assessment can be practised. A sample paper is provided on the website identifying some of the approaches that might be used.

The writing task is marked externally with a maximum of 60 marks. The candidates are then banded into four bands –high to low – for the purpose of determining who will be invited for interview. It should be noted that the results of this task is not the only fact in deciding invitations for interview.

History Aptitude Test (HAT)

The HAT is used in the selection of candidates for all degree courses involving History. The test examines the skills and potentialities required for the study of History, and provides an objective basis for comparing candidates.

In this test candidates are required to read two extracts (one from a work of History) and answer a total of four questions about them. These questions test comprehension of the arguments contained in the extracts and the candidate's ability to think, make judgements and provide thoughtful interpretations. The

HAT is 2 hours in duration and does not require 'substantive historical knowledge' but candidates are expected to display some historical knowledge to illustrate and develop concepts or hypotheses.

Mathematics, Joint Schools and Computer Science

For candidates applying for Mathematics, Mathematics and Statistics, Computer Science, Mathematics and Computer Science, or Mathematics and Philosophy.

Multiple-choice question paper containing seven questions of which five should be attempted. The time allowed for this test is 2 hours. There are extra sheets included in the booklet for rough work. And the use of calculators or formula sheets is prohibited.

History and Economics

For candidates applying for the joint school of History and Economics.

This is a written test that is conducted at the time of the interview. It comprises one numerical and one critical reasoning question and candidates are allowed 15 minutes preliminary reading time and 30 minutes for writing.

Fine Art

For candidates of Fine Art the test is held at the Ruskin School of Drawing and Fine Art.

Candidates are required to make three drawings in any medium, choosing the subject from a list provided at the time of the test. Materials such as paper, card, ink, tape, glue, scissors, pencils and charcoal are provided. There are two examination sessions on the same day, a morning session of 2 hours and an afternoon session of 3 hours.

Psychology

For candidates applying for Experimental Psychology and the joint school of Psychology, Philosophy and Physiology.

This is a written test that is conducted at the time of the interview. The test normally comprises a written article and four questions based on that article and candidates are allowed 15 minutes preliminary reading time and 1 hour for writing.

Physics Aptitude Test (PAT)

For candidates applying for Physics, and Physics and Philosophy.

The PAT is conducted at the time of the interview and is in three parts: Section A is multiple-choice with 10 questions; Section B requires written answers; Section C is a long question. All the questions must be attempted and the time allowed for the test is 1 hour. Calculators may be used but not tables.

Philosophy and Theology – Philosophy and Modern Languages

This is a written test that is conducted at the time of the interview. Candidates are required to write two essays selecting one question from Part A and one question from Part B. The time allowed for the test is half an hour for each essay.

Classics

For candidates applying for Literae Humaniores Course II, Classics and English with preliminary Course II year, and Classics and Modern Languages (after Classics Honour Mods Course II). The Language Aptitude Test is conducted at the time of the interview and the time allowed is 1 hour.

For candidates applying for Literae Humaniores Courses IC and II – the GCSE standard test in Latin or Greek, i.e. translation from Latin or Greek to English, and the time allowed is 1 hour.

For candidates applying for Literae Humaniores Course I, Classics and English, and Classics and Modern Languages (after Modern Languages Prelim. or Classics Mods) – the A Level standard test in Latin or Greek, i.e. translation from Latin or Greek to English, and the time allowed is 1 hour.